Listen to ME, satan!

Listen to ME, satan!

Carlos Annacondia

Charisma
HOUSE
A STRANG COMPANY

Most STRANG COMMUNICATIONS/CHARISMA HOUSE/CHRISTIAN LIFE/SILOAM/ FRONTLINE/EXCEL BOOKS/REALMS products are available at special quantity discounts for bulk purchase for sales promotions, premiums, fund-raising, and educational needs. For details, write Strang Communications/Charisma House/ Christian Life/Siloam/FrontLine/Excel Books/Realms, 600 Rinehart Road, Lake Mary, Florida 32746, or telephone (407) 333-0600.

LISTEN TO ME, SATAN! by Carlos Annacondia
Published by Charisma House
A Strang Company
600 Rinehart Road
Lake Mary, Florida 32746
www.strangdirect.com

Unless otherwise noted, all Scripture quotations are from the Holy Bible, New International Version. Copyright © 1973, 1978, 1984, International Bible Society. Used by permission.

Scripture quotations marked KJV are from the King James Version of the Bible.

Design Director: Bill Johnson
Cover Designer: Jerry Pomales

Copyright © 1998, 2008 by Carlos Annacondia
All rights reserved

International Standard Book Number: 978-1-59979-234-7

The Library of Congress has catalogued the previous edition as follows:

Library of Congress Cataloging-in-Publication Data:

Annacondia, Carlos, 1944—
    [¡Oíme bien, Satanás! English]
    Listen to me, Satan! / Carlos Annacondia with Gisela Sawin: translated by Silvia Cudich.
        p. cm.
    ISBN: 0-88419-524-4 (pbk.)
    1. Annacondia, Carlos, 1944— . 2. Evangelists—Argentina. 3. Spiritual life. 4. Miracles. I. Sawin, Gisela. II. Title.
BV3785.A64A3   1998
269.2'092—dc21
[B]
                                                                98-21052
                                                                CIP

Previously published as ¡Oíme bien, Satanás! by Betania, un sello de Editorial Caribe, copyright © 1997, ISBN: 0-88113-438-4

08 09 10 11 12 — 98765432
Printed in the United States of America

Dedication

I dedicate this book to my Lord and Father, to Jesus Christ, and to the Holy Spirit, the only author of these pages;

to my loving wife, María, my helpmate and mother of my nine children—together we bear the load (or burden) of the ministry;

to my mother for her faithful prayers;

to Pastor Manuel A. Ruiz of Panama, who reached me with the gospel message; Pastors Jorge Gomelsky and Pedro Ibarra, who in different stages of our Christian walk God used to strengthen our lives in Christ.

I especially dedicate this to all who have a passion for lost souls and have a desire for God to use them. I pray the Lord uses this book as an instrument of inspiration for those people.

Acknowledgments

I would like to thank my co-workers in the ministry
Mensaje de Salvación [Message of Salvation];

the pastors who day after day support our crusades;

the intercessors;

all those who support the ministry with their gifts
so we can continue winning souls for Christ;

and I also want to thank those who filled the
pages of this book with their testimonies.

Contents

Part Four: "They Will Speak in New Tongues…"

Part Five: "Deadly Poison Will Not Hurt Them…"

Part Six: "Sick People Will Get Well…"

Foreword

THE AMAZING ARGENTINE REVIVAL, AT THIS WRITING, IS finishing its fifteenth year! This is quite notable because even the most famous revivals—like the Azusa Street Revival, the Welsh Revival, or the Great Awakening—lasted only a couple of years. It is true that the long-term effects, the afterglow, of some lasted much longer, but the revival fire itself was relatively short-lived.

Carlos Annacondia is the most visible and most widely recognized apostle of the Argentine Revival. He is joined by other outstanding servants of God such as Omar Cabrera, Claudio Freidzon, Pablo Deiros, Edgardo Silvoso, Pablo Bottari, Eduardo Lorenzo, and, more recently, Sergio Scataglini. The consensus is that the revival was sparked when Carlos Annacondia began his public evangelistic ministry in 1982.

The widespread outpouring of the Holy Spirit that we have been praying for seems right around the corner. Never before have so many Christians been talking about revival, preaching about revival, offering courses and seminars on revival, and writing books and articles on revival.

Make no mistake about it. *Listen to Me, Satan!* may well be regarded by future historians as one of the most important if not the most important book of the revival literature of the 1990s. I am thrilled that it is now available in English.

Carlos and I have been friends for years. I have participated in his campaigns, ministered to his staff, traveled with him, translated for him, prayed with him, talked and written about him, and eaten Argentine beefsteak with him. There is no Christian leader whom I respect more. If there is ever any such thing as an Evangelists' Hall of Fame, Annacondia will be right there along with Billy Graham, Morris Cerullo, T. L. Osborn, Reinhard Bonnke, and the like. The only reason we have not heard more about him in America as yet is that he is not fluent in English.

My research has shown that the principal reasons why the Argentine Revival has lasted more than most revivals all relate to Annacondia. Annacondia has kept evangelism—winning lost souls—as the central focus for twenty-five years. He has insisted on evangelical unity wherever he has gone, and he has seen it happen. Many cities in Argentina divide their recent history as "before Annacondia" and "after Annacondia." Furthermore, he has knit his heart together with the other leaders, or apostles, of the Argentine Revival, overcoming the jealousy, indifference, competitiveness, bitterness, and divisions that have characterized so many similar movements.

No factor about the Argentine Revival is more significant than taking seriously the demonic forces that attempt to throttle evangelism and to quench revival. The title of this book is Carlos Annacondia's signature war cry, "Listen to me, Satan!" As I have seen with my own eyes, when he shouts this out in his public meetings, literally "all hell breaks loose!" Demons manifest, and the demonized victims are immediately taken out and ministered to one-on-one, sometimes through most of the night, by trained deliverance counselors.

This clears the air for the harvest. When Carlos gives the invitation, men and women from all levels of society actually run up front to get saved. It is no "eyes closed and heads bowed and let's sing another verse of 'Just As I Am'" scenario as most of us are used to. It is a free for all, frequently with shoving and pushing to get here first. So far, more than two million have reached the front, been saved, and have moved from darkness to light, from the power of Satan to God!

As you read this book, you will feel like you are there. My prayer is that God will move you to say, "Lord, I want to recommit myself to do my part for this kind of revival to come to my city and to my nation!"

—C. PETER WAGNER
FULLER THEOLOGICAL SEMINARY
1997

Preface

I T IS A GREAT PRIVILEGE FOR ME TO INTRODUCE THIS BOOK BY evangelist Carlos Annacondia. As a fellow countryman, I feel proud that Carlos, with his impeccable and crystal clear testimony, is an Argentinean ambassador who represents us so excellently all over the world.

Since 1983, his ministry has continued to grow and be effective for the kingdom of God by winning souls for Christ and mobilizing the church in pursuit of the Great Commission.

In the eighties, God raised Brother Carlos to be the spokesman of the message of salvation to a downhearted people defeated in their pride. He was the instrument chosen by God for a revival that shook all of Argentina. His faithfulness, his devotion, and his faith in signs and miracles produced an awakening in the church toward evangelization. Believers came out of their buildings with renewed enthusiasm to announce the good news, signaling a new time for our country. Today, his ministry extends over all the nations of the world.

I met Carlos Annacondia in 1983. At that time, I was a professor of theology in the *Instituto Bíblico Río de la Plata* [Bible Institute of the Río de la Plata], the seminary of the Assemblies of God in Argentina. Through my students, I found out about the evangelistic crusade taking place in the city of La Plata, located fifty kilometers from Buenos Aires. The evangelist was Carlos Annacondia, who was at that point starting his evangelistic ministry and whom I still didn't know. The remarks of those students who were helping in that crusade caught my attention. "What's happening is extraordinary; every night thousands of people accept Jesus Christ as their Savior, and the power of deliverance is so strong that we need to stay until very late at night praying for the demonized," they said. I then immediately decided: *I need to meet this man.*

That evening I went to the location of the crusade in La Plata. My students' report was surpassed by the reality before my eyes. A crowd surrounded the platform, and I could sense an atmosphere of great expectation. When the service began, the evangelist went up on the platform with his Bible in hand. As soon as he started talking, I felt the strong anointing of the Holy Spirit. Then came the prayer. It wasn't just any prayer—it had authority and seemed to electrify the atmosphere. "LISTEN TO ME, SATAN!" were the words that initiated the confrontation. From then on, in the name of Jesus, Brother Carlos directly rebuked all the powers and demons that could be affecting the audience.

It didn't take long for the prayer to have an effect. A lot of people fell down with loud shrieks, trembling and showing external manifestations that indicated spiritual problems in their lives. There were hundreds! The assistants carried some away to take care of them in a special place. The authority of Jesus was revealed there in an amazing way. Then came the preaching. And when Brother Annacondia gave the evangelistic call with a love that could only come from on high, the people started to run toward the platform. They were asking for their salvation with tears in their eyes. I left that place moved in my spirit, with a new vision burning in my heart.

In good time, we established a deep friendship. We started to meet together every Thursday with other pastors to pray and share our burden for the lost. I remember times in which we would put a map of Argentina right in the center of our group and ask God for a revival in every corner of the country. Those were indescribable moments of spiritual liveliness.

Carlos Annacondia is a man of God. His testimony of humility and love for souls is evident to all who meet him. It's impossible to be with him and not talk about God's work and our love for the lost.

This book will awaken you spiritually. The signs that accompany those who believe will become a reality in your life when you take hold of the authority given to you by God. Brother Carlos knows these subjects as very few people do. They are part of his experience, and he teaches them with authority.

Carlos Annacondia's ministry has challenged my life as a pastor. All those nights at the crusade filled my heart with their atmosphere of faith and miracles. I sincerely desire that the same will happen to you. Through this book, may you receive the burden and the power to be a faithful and victorious witness.

—CLAUDIO J. FREIDZON
PASTOR, *REY DE REYES* CHURCH, BUENOS AIRES, ARGENTINA

Introduction

IN THE FIRST YEAR AFTER I CAME TO KNOW JESUS CHRIST, I FELT a strong burden in my heart. My deepest prayer was for my country, since I felt that Argentina was losing itself. Every day I cried over a map of this nation, laying my hands on each province as I prayed for the lost souls there. I spent hours claiming Argentina for Christ.

Back then, the ministry of *Mensaje de Salvación* [Message of Salvation], directed by myself today, didn't yet exist, but God showed me books, many books, with my name in them. That was a very clear vision. In any case, I never rush into things; on the contrary, I always wait for God to push me. I constantly tell Him, "Lord, if this is of You, You will push me to do it." And so it happened that God drove me to write this book as He has done in every event of my life.

Only a few books other than the Bible have had an impact on my life. But I will never forget the time I read Kathryn Kuhlman's books. These books about miracles made me cry; each time a very strong urge compelled me to get on my knees and pray. Somehow I would say, "Lord, I want You to give me what that woman had." God has answered my prayer. And today I feel joy as I minister salvation to the lost and show them the way, the truth, and the life.

No matter what place you occupy in the body of Christ, it is my desire that through these pages you will reach a sphere where you will experience supernatural events. All the testimonies you will find here have a unique objective: to inspire and challenge you to search for the supernatural aspects of God.

It is my humble prayer, and my only purpose, that these pages will give you light to understand my message and that they will leave you with a different experience, a lasting impression in your life. It is not my intention to fill library shelves or to see my name printed in books. Success or fame does not motivate me. My only purpose is to bring to your life the blessing of discovering the affirmation of supernatural signs from God to all those who believe in Him. When you finish reading this book, may you be able to feel the same as I do so that we can come together to proclaim with one voice: *The world for Christ.*

Jesus said:

> Go into all the world and preach the good news to all creation. Whoever believes and is baptized will be saved, but whoever does not believe will be condemned. And these signs will accompany those who believe: In my name they will drive out demons; they will speak in new tongues; they will pick up snakes with their hands; and when they drink deadly poison, it will not hurt them at all; they will place their hands on sick people, and they will get well.
>
> —MARK 16:15–18

Part One

"GO . . . AND PREACH"

Chapter 1

GOD'S CALL

O N THE NIGHT OF MAY 26, 1984, FIVE EDITORS OF THE newspaper *El Guardián* attended our crusade in Ensenada, hiding discreetly in the crowd. They had heard stories of the amazing events taking place at our crusades. They were there to record the evidences they found of fraud in the supernatural miracles that God was allowing to take place. The following account from the newspaper shows that not only did they not find fraud, but that also with astonishment they recorded the miraculous healings they observed as they watched God move in power and glory.

MIRACULOUS HEALINGS AND INEXPLICABLE EVENTS IN ENSENADA

On the night of May 26, 1984, five editors of the newspaper *El Guardián* [The Guardian] were witnesses of some events whose paranormal spectacularity and veracity don't accept any kind of objections. Spread in between the four thousand people assembled around the stage at the evangelical church...the journalists saw over three hundred people fall as if struck by lightning by the mere touch of the Christian preacher Carlos Annacondia's hands and, at the time, also verified healings....

Of the five professionals [editors] at that place, three were Catholic, one was a nominal Christian, and the other an atheist.... Right before the eyes of this group used to analyzing events and

5

things with a total impartiality in judgment and cold reasoning were ladies foaming at the mouth, children fallen on the wet grass, women collapsed in the mud—three of them wearing expensive fur coats—and hundreds of young people both male and female, old people, and men of humble condition, stumbling as they made efforts not to fall. Nothing we are saying is exaggerated....

All the faces of those "touched" by the evangelist Annacondia showed visible expressions of pain or happiness, none of which could be alleged as a fictitious dramatization; these were very simple people incapable of any setups or of receiving it through telepathy with such fidelity. It suggested biblical days, hours lived by the early church, but not a premeditated act performed to deceive unsuspecting people.

Annacondia is not a hypnotist...he uses the Word of God as a direct transmitter and doesn't separate from it. None of his phrases moves a bit away from the Gospels...he doesn't claim to heal anybody since it is "God who heals." And the healings are many. A reporter from *El Guardián* who suffered an injury in his left knee's cartilage, due to a bad fall, stopped feeling any pain and could move his leg (he had been like that for three months)....

The almost thirty thousand people who went through the different nights of the ministry, over and against the investigators and reporters' opinions, emerge as a solid witness that inexplicable but real things happened every night of prayer, nights in which they spoke about Christ and God—and about Them only.

As the newspapers recorded, each crusade night is extraordinary. Worship songs fill the auditorium, and raised hands reveal a desire to worship the Lord. The people happily express the supernatural miracles that take place in their lives.

One woman caught my attention in a special way and moved me deeply. That woman had experienced a miracle, and she told us the following story about her miracle:

> I lived all my childhood with my parents and three brothers and sisters at a place in the country where the Río Dulce intersects with several streams. This place is located at the border between the provinces of Córdoba and Santiago del Estero.
>
> One afternoon as she opened a big trunk, a snake bit my mother in several parts of her body. Desperate and experiencing intense

pain, she fell crying right in front of us. Our father didn't do anything, and although my eldest brother screamed at him for help, he didn't react. Soon after, I saw my father preparing the horse-drawn carriage and driving away, leaving my mother lying on the ground dying and us alone at her side. With great effort we placed my mother on the bed, but she was very sick. It was almost dark, so we decided to take her in a canoe to a place where we could get help. It was useless. She died.

There we were, the four of us together before our mother's dead body and alone. The youngest of my brothers and sisters was Juan; he was only eleven months old. Then there was me, four years old. My sister, Juana, was five, and finally, Pedro, my oldest brother, was eight years old.

We built a coffin with our own hands to bury my mother, and with the help of a neighbor who came to see us, we took her to the cemetery. The closest person lived a day and a half away on horseback. We supposed that this neighbor came to us because our father, when he left, managed to tell him about our situation. After burying my mother, our neighbor left. He promised to come back but never did.

We were alone. We went back to our adobe house and there we lived, left to our fate. Every afternoon we went back to the cemetery because we felt that since my mother's body was there, we were protected. We did this every day for three years. We were not afraid; this was our home. Actually, we felt so comfortable there that we used to play and sleep among the tombs.

Today, I realize that God protected us all during that time when we were by ourselves. We ate fish and hunted by installing good traps. There were many ducks, eggs, sheep, and some other things available to us. We gave our little brother, Juan, milk from a goat that was nursing her own kids; the goat would lie down and Juan would crawl to feed directly from her. Our oldest brother was the one in charge of the food, although we all helped.

One day, my eldest brother made us swear that the first one of us who had the opportunity would kill our father. We were practically savages. We were naked, dirty, and unkempt. The only thing that kept us alive was the desire to kill our father. That gave us the strength we needed to survive.

Three years later, our father came back home, tied us up, put us in bags, and took us to the nearest town. There he gave us away to different landowners, separating us despite our great love for each other.

The ranchers that took me taught me how to work the land, make bread, and some other tasks. Although I was only seven years old, I worked very hard. They practically had to tame me. But even there, the pact I had made with my brothers and sister to kill my father was the thing that continued to give me the strength to live. I had to grow up so that I could execute vengeance on behalf of my mother. I never saw my brothers and my sister again, but the hope of finding them also helped me to live.

When I was fourteen, the son of the family that brought me up raped me and hit me fiercely. One day, tired of enduring all that he did to me, I told his parents everything. They said I was lying and hit me so badly that I ended up in the hospital for three months. The doctors said that I failed to get better because I didn't want to live.

A fever continued to waste me away, but when I remembered our pact, I slowly began to get well until I was able to go back to work at the ranch. One night before I turned seventeen, I ran away, hid in the fields of sorghum, walked to the closest town, arriving before dawn. I ran to the police station and told them what had happened to me. But they put me in one of the cells where two policemen hit and raped me.

I really wanted to die. Even the town's chief of police wanted to rape me that night, but I threw myself at his feet and begged him not to do it. "Please stop hurting me," I pleaded. He felt sorry for me and left me alone. He told me that the family that had raised me was a very powerful one in that region and that I should go back to them. I told him that my real father was also well known and suggested that he find him; surely he would give the chief of police some money for my release. Finally the captain agreed, and he notified the family and, at the same time, my father about my whereabouts.

That same day I went back to my father. He had never seen my brothers and sister since he left us years earlier. I was happy to find him. Now I could finally kill him. I was the first one to stand before him. I was a young girl that could handle knives very well, and I saw the opportunity to carry out what we had promised to each other so many years before.

My father was in a good financial situation. He tried to talk to me, to make me feel comfortable, but I would not respond. I repeatedly showed him my knives, telling him: "Don't go to sleep because one of those nights I am going to kill you."

Day after day, I did not sit at the same table with my father for lunch and dinner. I took my plate outside the house to eat on the ground, using my fingers, demonstrating to my father what he had done to me. Seeing this, he would cry and ask for forgiveness, but I was filled with hatred toward him.

One day I took a knife and decided to kill him. I wanted it to be face-to-face so I could see his suffering. I lunged at him with the knife. I thought I had killed him, but when I looked at the knife I didn't see any blood. So I told him, "Dad, your time has not come yet, but I will kill you soon."

One afternoon as I was eating outside in the patio, I heard a very loud noise, like something falling. That sound made me shudder, and I perceived the smell of death. My father had fallen dead. In part I was happy, although I had wished to kill him with my own hands.

My father's death gave way to new torments, since now I didn't know what to do with my life as an orphan. A young man who was acquainted with my father came to see me and offered to marry me. I accepted so I could have somebody to take care of me. But the misfortunes continued. My husband abused me, he didn't want to work, and he treated me like one of the servants.

When I became pregnant, he took me to Buenos Aires and left me with a family. They treated me miserably. My torture was such that one afternoon I decided to throw myself under a passing train, but miraculously the train stopped right in front of me.

Before our son was born, my husband came back to get me, but the suffering continued. I ran away again to go live in the city of Rosario with my two children, a boy of two and a one-month-old girl. It was difficult to live and work there. Finally my husband found me and came to live with us.

In 1985, a neighbor told me about Annacondia's crusade. There I gave my life to the Lord, but there were no changes in me.

Some years later I got sick. I had bad hemorrhages, and I wasn't getting any better. In 1991 I decided to look for an evangelical church. That seed planted by Brother Annacondia was finally germinating.

I went to church with my whole family. I started going regularly, but there was no forgiveness in my heart, and I would not talk about my previous life. My past was hidden in my heart. Even though I served at my church and was a disciplined worker, I had never been able to forgive everyone who had hurt me so badly.

When they announced in 1996 that Carlos Annacondia was going to hold a crusade in my city, I got ready to work as an assistant in the service of the Lord. A few nights before the crusade started, I told God that I wanted to be a good worker. "If there is anything in me that needs Your cleansing, please show it to me," I prayed. I also asked Him for the opportunity to be able to find my brothers and sister. I knew that my sister was in Santa Fe, but I had never found her. I prayed for her constantly.

One morning at ten o'clock before the beginning of the crusade, I was given a letter from Juan, my youngest brother. Immediately I got hold of him by phone, and a few days later I went to the city to see him.

I thanked the Lord so much for helping me to find my brother, and many times I asked Him to forgive me for all the wrong things I had done.

During that last crusade, while Brother Annacondia was preaching about the barriers that prevent God's blessings from reaching us, I was able to forgive from my heart. I saw something like angels flying all around me and God's hand removing all hatred and resentment from my life. I cried out so loud from the depths of my soul, asking God to forgive me for everything I had plotted against my father and husband, that I eventually lost my voice. I was able to forgive them from the very depths of my being, which helped me to find healing for my broken heart. Although I had known God for several years, I had never been able to really forgive. That barrier, that unforgiveness, had prevented His blessing from reaching my life.

God removed the hatred I had toward men, and He removed the rejection I felt from my husband. He removed the bitterness from my heart, gave me new strength, and above all, He restored my marriage.

I give God all the glory and all the honor for the changes He brought into my life, and for His servant, His chosen instrument— Carlos Annacondia—who brought me to the knowledge of the truth.

—CARMEN

This woman's testimony had an impact not only on her life but also on the lives of many others who listened to her story. Along with her story, many other testimonies were shared from the platform. My astonishment and admiration for the awesome and supernatural power of God never ceases to grow.

As I was thanking God that night for all the miracles that had taken place, I understood His purposes through my life and His will for my calling.

I still don't understand why, but ever since I was a young boy—even though I hadn't received God in my heart—I always knew that somebody mightier whom I couldn't see was taking care of me. A few times I told some of my friends about this feeling.

Just like so many other Argentineans, I come from a family of immigrants, Spanish on my mother's side, Italian on my father's. I was raised according to the Italian culture. My grandfather, a typical Italian, used to teach me, "The man who cries is not a man. If somebody hits you, don't come to me crying; fight back." These and so many other teachings gave shape to my life since I was a little boy.

My parents were very humble. When I was a young boy, we lived in a tenement house together—my parents, my two brothers—Angel, the oldest; the youngest, José María—and me in the middle. My father worked for the electric company, and my mother took care of us.

Everything changed when my father fell terribly ill, and we had to go out to work. I was only ten years old, but every morning I got up early to go to work in a butcher's shop. After working there all day and cleaning the place up, I came back home, leaving for night school soon after. Many mornings when I got up, I told my mom that my stomach was hurting, when in reality I just didn't want to go to work. My mother used to prepare me a cup of tea and then send me to work. That's how I learned to be responsible, and therefore I started to grow up.

The Book of Proverbs says, "Lazy hands make a man poor, but diligent hands bring wealth" (Prov. 10:4). Everything I undertook prospered. Everybody liked me. Even when I served in the military at twenty years of age, I was sent to work in the best place. Nobody could figure out what I had done to be there. They gave me the best tasks to perform and promoted me to higher military rankings. I was always ahead of my peers.

When I was twenty-one years old, I met María, my wife, who was only fifteen. My grandfather used to tell me to look for a young girlfriend so I could train her well. We got married when I was twenty-five and she was nineteen. Back then, my brother and I were starting the company where I still work today.

Time went by, and there was a great void in my life; there was fear in my heart. My goal in life was to have peace and happiness, and I thought I could achieve these things by being successful and recognized at work. Therefore, I worked a lot, believing that by amassing goods and making money I would finally be happy. When I was thirty-five I obtained the solid financial status I had always wanted. Together with my two brothers, we had created the most important company of its type in our country. I could buy anything I wanted and give my wife, María, and my four children whatever they asked for. So supposedly and according to my way of thinking, I should have been a happy man.

I still felt that huge void, however, and I realized I was terribly mistaken. None of the things I had obtained with great effort could bring me peace or happiness. Every weekend, burdened by my problems, María and I would get the children ready and go to a summer resort on the Atlantic Ocean, looking for some peace and quiet. But when I would come back to work, I would feel worse than before. I didn't sleep at night, and I had fears, insecurities, and worries. I was afraid of life itself, of death, of sickness, of losing all I had, of something terrible happening to my children. I even felt guilty for having brought them into this world full of wars, violence, and drugs. So I decided in my heart not to have any more children.

Every month that went by, every year, I only felt worse. I had every reason to be happy, and yet I wasn't. I wondered where peace and happiness could be found; I started to think they were a mere invention of the mind.

At that time, I was part of a group of prestigious businessmen. In every meeting I wasn't introduced simply as Carlos but as the owner of such and such company. They didn't care about the real person. They were only interested in what I owned. I started to notice the lack of honesty that existed in that kind of relationship, and I pulled apart from those who called themselves my friends.

Until then I had never worried about God, although I had been baptized and married in a Catholic church. I believed in a distant God, indifferent to those who could only talk to Him through an intermediary. I didn't know God cared about me and wanted to have a personal relationship with me. I also didn't know that I could become His friend and get to know Him and have intimacy with Him.

But one day in 1979 I heard the good news. I heard a God who says, "Come to me, all you who are weary and burdened, and I will give you rest" (Matt. 11:28). I was invited to a meeting where Reverend Manuel Ruiz, the Panamanian ambassador in Bolivia at the time, was preaching. During the meeting I realized that what the preacher was saying was directly addressed to me, to my heart. He said, "You are loaded with fears, insecurities, and failures. All these things are before the eyes of God. Give your heart to Him, and He will take care not only of your family but also of all your problems."

When I heard those words, I started to cry like I hadn't been able to cry in years. Listening to the voice of God through one of His servants, I realized that God loved me, that He had remembered me. When the preacher asked how many people needed God, I raised my hand because I really needed Him with all my heart. I asked my wife, who was sitting right next to me, if she also wanted to accept Jesus. She answered me, "I have been waiting a long time for this."

As I lifted my hand, it felt as if it weighed a ton. All kinds of thoughts were rushing through my mind. What would my friends, my family, or the businessmen at the club say? What would the bank managers with whom I worked think? And what about the merchandise managers and other businessmen? Would they mock me or laugh at me because of my decision to receive Christ in my heart? But before me was One bigger than all of them put together.

On the night of May 19, 1979, at exactly ten thirty, María and I accepted Jesus into our hearts. I will never forget what happened when we left that meeting. As we came out, everything seemed different. I had not been able to buy peace or happiness with money or success. But Christ gave it all to me as a gift just because He loved me. Nothing in my life ever had brought such an extraordinary change as the one that took place when I lifted my hands to God. Every day that went by I felt happier. I stopped smoking and drinking; I left all my doubts and fears behind. I had been addicted to TV, but since the day I met Christ I somehow forgot to watch it. Everything had changed.

After coming to know the Lord, we had five more children. Today my family consists of my wife, my nine children, and several grandchildren. Our children are Carlos Alberto, Angel, María Eugenia, José María, Rebecca, Moisés, Elías, Rut, and Natanael. Today, we are really happy.

Since María and I became Christians in a crusade, we didn't have a local church that we could attend. That's why we decided, along with other families who had given their lives to the Lord in that same crusade, to start meeting together.

Together with us were several employees from our company: our sales manager, the person in charge of one of our departments, and a few others. We looked for a pastor who could lead us. None of us knew how to preach, but the Lord placed a pastor in our midst. During that first period, Pastor Gomelski helped us grow. Together with him we created a vision to win souls for Christ. We were so enthusiastic that with very little knowledge of God's Word, we preached to everybody, sharing our own experiences. Our faith was simple and had no structure, yet people were still being healed and saved. Our most important message was that of the good news of our Lord Jesus Christ and His love for us. We prayed for the sick, believing that they were going to get healed—and they did. We preached salvation, having no doubts that the person in front of us was going to accept the Lord.

When we founded our church in 1979, we were all new converts. We began with four couples and their children. We were the church's workers, the elders, and the deacons. But God filled that place very rapidly.

A week after my conversion, I received the promise of the baptism of the Holy Spirit with His sign of speaking in tongues. God gave me a vision: I saw a stadium filled with people, and I saw myself preaching in a language I did not understand. From that moment on, I started to feel a burden for the people who didn't know Christ. I preached about the Lord to whoever would cross my way.

Even though I was still working, the most important thing in my life was serving the Lord, not making money. This was a difficult situation for the members of my family who didn't know the Lord and couldn't accept that my life was devoted to Him. They tried to persuade me to see my "mistake," quoting the advice of my most intelligent and important friends. These encounters always ended with my testifying to them and their turning their lives over to the Lord.

During those first days of my walk with the Lord, something astounding was happening to me. During my times of prayer, God always showed me the shantytowns. At night when I closed my eyes, I could see poor areas that were shunned by society: children going barefoot and houses made of cardboard and corrugated iron roofs.

At first I could not understand what God meant, and I thought I had to leave or give away my possessions, including my share of the company—simply give everything to the poor. I felt burdened by the Lord and spent many days praying and crying, not finding any peace. When I prayed with María concerning this, the Holy Spirit touched her and she said, "I am with you." But I couldn't find any comfort.

One afternoon I told María, "I want to leave everything behind and move to the Chaco to preach in the jungle. Do you want to come with me?"

Her response was, "I'll go wherever you go."

That same afternoon I left my home and decided to give everything away. The first thing I did was give my father my brand-new car since he needed one.

Then I went to talk to my pastor, Brother Gomelski. After giving some thought to what I was telling him, he said, "You have worked very hard to obtain what you have; you didn't steal it. Therefore, use your assets for God only when He asks you to."

That moment I felt as Abraham did when he lifted his knife, ready to kill his son. When God saw that His servant didn't hesitate but was willing to carry out His orders, even handing over his own son, God stopped Abraham's hand. God realized that my treasure was not composed of my material belongings but of my love for Him and for the lost. Today I realize that it would have been a mistake to give up everything, since for many people, including my family, it would have been more of a scandal than a blessing.

"I'm Giving You What You Have Requested"

One day, two and one-half years after my conversion, our pastor brought me an invitation to preach in a very humble church in the city of La Plata in the province of Buenos Aires. Taking the given invitation in my hands, I felt something very special from God in my heart, and I therefore accepted.

The church was so poor that it had no floors—just pieces of old carpet lying on the ground. The congregation was composed of twenty-five people. That night after preaching, the Holy Spirit came in such power that everybody in the place received the baptism of the Holy

Spirit. At the end of the meeting, the pastor's wife approached me, saying, "God spoke to me and said that the person preaching tonight is going to be the one to bring a revival to the city of La Plata. The sign is going to be the outpouring of the Holy Spirit filling everybody with God's power."

There weren't too many people in that meeting, but two brothers from a church from the city of Berisso, a place close to La Plata, were present. They invited me to arrange for a crusade in their church. That is how I started to preach. After that first crusade, because a large amount of crusades were being organized, we put together a working team that we called *Mensaje de Salvación* [Message of Salvation].

On April 12, 1982, God spoke to me in an audible voice. He said, "Read the vision of the valley of dry bones in Ezekiel 37. From now on I will give you what you have requested."

My prayer had been "Argentina for Christ." I wanted Him to show supernatural signs in my country so that people would come to know Him. I wasn't born in a desert or in a jungle, but in a place where millions of people lived, yet nobody had ever talked to me about Jesus. I didn't hear about Him until somebody told me about the supernatural signs taking place in the crusade where I was converted. It was these signs that drove me to the place where I met the Lord. Then I understood that if there were no signs of God in Argentina, people would not believe. In the Gospels, supernatural signs are not for the *believers* but for the *unbelievers*. In my country, "seeing is believing" is a must.

As I read Ezekiel 37, I understood that it was the breath of the Holy Spirit that would bring about the miracles.

> Then he said to me, "Prophesy to these bones and say to them, 'Dry bones, hear the word of the LORD!'"…Then he said to me, "Prophesy to the breath; prophesy, son of man, and say to it, 'This is what the Sovereign LORD says: Come from the four winds, O breath, and breathe into these slain, that they may live.'" So I prophesied as he commanded me, and breath entered them; they came to life and stood up on their feet—a vast army.
>
> —EZEKIEL 37:4, 9–10

People started to hear about *Mensaje de Salvación* [Message of Salvation] because of all the miracles that took place during our meetings. People ran to the platform to receive the Lord. Today I can assure you that not everything I had to go through in response to my calling was easy. There were things happening in my life that I couldn't understand.

When I received the baptism of the Holy Spirit something happened. The brothers who were present that night saw something special from God over me. Some time later during a service, the pastor asked me if I could help him pray for the sick. When I started to pray, people began falling one after the other. The falling was not something foreign to me. I had seen people falling in the crusade led by the Panamanian evangelist. But I was surprised when I realized it was actually happening to me. For a while after, I stopped praying for others until God spoke to me directly saying He wanted to use me.

At that time I went to buy a car. The owner of the vehicle opened his front door, and as he was showing it to me, suddenly something happened. Inside his home, his wife and daughter started manifesting demons. The wife started to break things around the house. The husband went in and was finally able to stop her. An evil spirit had been tormenting these women for some time. The man told me later that they had been believers who had turned their backs to God and made many mistakes.

After that incident, I realized that nothing depended on me. That woman had manifested demons, and I didn't even know she was inside the house. What happened was beyond my control. But then God gave me something special so that no matter where I was, He who lives in my heart would express Himself and make the devil flee. I then realized that I wasn't the one in control of the situation—God was. And so I yielded myself entirely to Him.

Part Two

"THESE SIGNS WILL ACCOMPANY THOSE WHO BELIEVE..."

Chapter 2

ANOINTING IN THE MINISTRY

God's work is enjoying fruitful times not only in Argentina but also in many regions in America as well. People hunger for God; they have a need to find the right path. I believe that it is necessary for us to be well prepared, and for that reason we need God's anointing to support our ministries. Every work that doesn't have God's anointed signature is as good as dead.

Even those who don't have Christ in their lives should be able to recognize the anointing. As we walk through our days, when we are at work or performing different activities, those around us should see something different in us. Even though they don't express it with the same words as we do, this "something" is called *anointing*. If the world doesn't see that anointing in us, they won't believe that God has sent us. Our best training comes from the Holy Spirit. Without His work in our lives it would be impossible to do the will of God here on Earth. That's why it is necessary to be invested, filled, and permanently renewed by the power and grace of the Holy Spirit.

That was the case of a young woman who desperately wanted to find God. The merciful hand of God guided her to somebody who, without really knowing her, showed her the way of salvation. She tells about her beautiful testimony in this way:

"Don't Take Away What You Have Given Me"

I had a lot of problems in my life, and I decided I was going to commit suicide. For that reason, I always carried a letter in my purse explaining my decision. I had no knowledge of the evangelistic crusade beginning in the city of Mar del Plata. I didn't know the evangelist, Carlos Annacondia. I had never heard his name.

At the time I was the personnel manager in an important hotel in the city. But I had been sick and depressed for years even though I had a good family. I didn't lack a thing, but something was wrong inside of me.

One afternoon as I was waiting at work for my employees to change shifts, I suddenly decided to bring my life to an end. That was the day I had chosen to commit suicide. Since the place where I worked was located right in front of the ocean, I thought I would walk straight into the water without looking back and in that way put an end to all my sufferings.

The entrance to the hotel is very beautiful. It has big glass and bronze doors. From there one can hear the typical lobby's noise. Even though I was very used to those sounds, that afternoon I was surprised by the penetrating sound of the doors opening and closing. Suddenly, I felt a very strong hand grab my back and lift me up. I started to walk toward a person who was coming in through those big doors. As I approached him, I grabbed his shirt and said, "Sir, sir, could there be anybody who could tell me about God? I need somebody to tell me about Him."

That man, with very pure eyes and a very tender smile said to me, "Yes, I can tell you about God. I can tell you about a Christ who loves you and can save you. He is Jesus of Nazareth."

I will never forget those words. In that very moment, I started to ask the Lord to forgive me. I confessed all the sins I had ever committed, even those of my childhood. As I asked God for forgiveness, a light penetrated my being, and I started thanking Him. Then I looked at the man in front of me and said, "Tell me, who are you?"

"I am a servant of the Lord. I am evangelist Carlos Annacondia," he replied.

"I don't know you," I said, "but please don't take away what you just gave me."

Fifteen minutes later my husband came to pick me up, and he couldn't recognize me. From that day on, my life changed; I was never the same. That night I went to Annacondia's crusade, and there I gave my life to God right in front of a great crowd. Today I can say that I was the first person to give my life to the Lord through the evangelist in that first and unforgettable crusade in Mar del Plata.

Three days after I gave my life to the Lord, He spoke to me in an audible voice and told me that I was going to have another daughter. It wasn't an easy thing to understand or even accept, since I had had surgery and the surgeon had removed part of my reproductive organs. The doctors told me that I wasn't able to have any more children. I was thirty-seven years old and had three daughters. But today my fourth girl is eleven years old and is the result of having believed God.

Shortly after that crusade, God called me to serve Him. Today I work for Him. My husband and I are pastors at an annex of our church. God is our inspiration and our strength.

—MARÍA

Without God's anointing, no ministry on Earth can be successful. If there is something we all need, it is what Jesus told His disciples: "Stay in the city until you have been clothed with power from on high" (Luke 24:49). The disciples first had to be filled with the power of God in order to be witnesses in Jerusalem, in Samaria, and finally to the ends of the earth. When we are invested with power, we have the ability to be witnesses, and that is how our ministries begin. There is where we will see the signs that will lead our way.

One day, a brother came to our church to invite somebody to preach and lead a three-day crusade in one of the shantytowns. There were several good preachers in our congregation; any one of them could do it. Nevertheless, this brother insisted that it was me who had to take the Word, since, in a vision, his wife had seen me preaching.

I had told God that I was never going to offer to preach in a crusade. It must always be He who sent people to invite me. In that way I could recognize when God was in it. And that's how it's been to this day.

By then God had already been talking to me, telling me that if I wanted Him to use me, I only had to believe. There, at the crusade in a shantytown, He would show me the real meaning of Mark 16:17. He told me the secret to supernatural signs—*to believe.*

The crusade I was invited to was in the midst of one of the most dangerous shantytowns in the area. The first night, several demonized gang members fell on the ground, rolling around and foaming at the mouth. They were all delivered from demonic bondage. The next day, they were the first ones there waiting for the meeting to start.

The second night of the crusade, some gang members switched off the electricity. But that didn't stop us. The brothers and I started to worship God with all our hearts, and the Holy Spirit fell in such a way that those standing at my right fell to the ground. Half of them started to roll around. I could see people coming in from the street shouting, others crying, some crawling, and I saw some hitting their heads against the pulpit, screaming. In the meantime, we all continued to worship until the electrical damage was repaired. That night I saw the work of the Holy Spirit convicting people of their sins, healing and delivering many.

On the third day of the crusade, evil spirits were still coming out of many of the people. Some people brought neighbors who were manifesting spirits in their own homes. That night, the meeting came to a close with an abundance of signs and wonders. This was only my first evangelistic crusade. The glory of God was there, showing signs that backed up His Word.

In a way similar to what happened to that woman in Mar del Plata, the world is waiting for somebody to preach to them, to bring them salvation, healing, and deliverance. The Bible tells us:

> As the Scripture says, "Anyone who trusts in him will never be put to shame." For there is no difference between Jew and Gentile—the same Lord is Lord of all and richly blesses all who call on him, for, "Everyone who calls on the name of the Lord will be saved."
>
> How, then, can they call on the one they have not believed in? And how can they believe in the one of whom they have not heard? And how can they hear without someone preaching to them? And how can they preach unless they are sent? As it is written, "How beautiful are the feet of those who bring good news!"
>
> —ROMANS 10:11–15

Have you, my dear friend, or your ministry heard the challenge of this mandate? If so, never forget the seven steps for appropriating the anointing into your ministry.

SEVEN STEPS FOR THE ANOINTING

There are seven requirements to be successful in Christian ministry. They are the basic elements for achieving an anointed and successful ministry. Without them, our service will be insignificant and unfruitful. They are as follows:

1. Consecration

By this I mean the total yielding to God. None of us are capable of developing a successful ministry without surrendering our whole life to Him.

In my company, when we need to hire someone to come and work for us, we put an ad in the newspaper. Many respond. They have to pass different tests according to the position available. We will choose the one whom we believe to be best equipped for the job. Yet, we don't do this without first evaluating certain conditions: for example, his or her capacity to perform the job and that person's experience.

In general, when it needs a minister, a servant, a co-worker, or an assistant, the church looks for a theologian who knows the Scriptures really well, someone with wisdom, skills, and experience. But what does God look for in a servant? His only requirement is a life entirely surrendered to Him. God doesn't look for a theologian or a wise man or woman or a dogmatic. God looks not only for abilities or wisdom but also for consecration and a total and complete surrender to Him. This isn't something easy to achieve. It's a struggle that demands our constant, total surrender, and it will require many other things that are hard for us to do.

I remember when God called me to the ministry. The first year I struggled with God because I had only surrendered 90 percent of my life to Him. I had received the baptism of the Holy Spirit, had been going to the hospitals to pray for the sick (who were being healed), had been preaching, and people were being converted; but in spite of all of this, there was a part of me that wasn't totally surrendered to the Lord.

I remember that many had prophesied about the ministry that God had given me. They told me that He was going to send me to other countries, that I was going to be an international evangelist, that all America would hear my voice, and many other things. Yet, I didn't sense a complete freedom in my life to develop this ministry.

One day, God showed me a shantytown in a dream. I asked myself: "Could it be that God wants me to go there and preach?" My immediate reaction was, "No... I'm not going there." Once again God showed me a shantytown in a dream. Again I said, "I'm not going there. How can I go to the shantytowns?" That was my struggle—I thought I was going to preach to the rich and famous, but God wanted me to preach to the poor.

I was feeling pretty bad when I realized what God was showing me and how I was responding. One day I told my wife, María, "If I decide to give everything away to go to the north of Argentina to preach the gospel with only what we have on our backs, would you follow me?"

She answered, "If this is what you sense God is telling you to do, I will come with you. I will follow you wherever you go."

I really thought that was what God wanted, until I finally understood that His will was for me to preach Christ in those places to those people. I soon realized that I wasn't interested in my material possessions any longer. I had lost the unhealthy love I had had for my company, which, until that moment, had been my life. When I removed the *I* and changed the priorities in my heart, He sent me to evangelize the poor.

We preached in the most outlying sectors of the city, under the rain, in the middle of the mud. That's how the ministry started. There I held crusades among thieves, perverts, and every kind of sin. María and I had rain boots in the car for the rainy days when we had to walk in those streets full of mud. But we preached with such joy!

God needed my total surrender. That's the first step. If there isn't a total surrender, He can't use us. It's not only about our conversion or the baptism of the Holy Spirit; God wants a life entirely consecrated to Him. He is looking for one who will say, "Lord, wherever You send me, I will go."

2. Vision

The second step to the anointing point is vision. What is the ministry vision that God has given to you? Within Christ's church there are five important ministry callings: apostle, prophet, evangelist, pastor, and teacher. I don't believe we are all called to be pastors or all called to be evangelists; then we would be building a deformed body. If God hasn't given you a ministry vision for your life yet, ask Him for one! You need to know your God-given call so you can set your eyes on that target. You need a clear and precise vision of the ministry you are going to develop. If not, it will be very hard to achieve it. There is a very specific calling for each one of us that we need to fulfill. When we have that calling, God gives us the vision, the shape, and the equipping of the Holy Spirit for us to be able to carry it on.

Do you know the most serious problem that the church faces today? *Triumphalism* (the belief that one doctrine, attitude, or belief is superior to all others). Careful! It is a disease that corrodes the ministries. Why do I say this? Very simply, if a pastor has a church of three thousand souls, anything less than that would be considered a failure. So in order to achieve that number of participants, he will do whatever it takes—be it the purchase of a big auditorium, two hours on the radio, borrowed money, or whatever—all for the simple purpose of having a church of three thousand members. That is *triumphalism.*

In reality, not all of God's callings are the same. Therefore, if you don't get the vision right, your ministry will fail. The important thing is to know what God's will is for our lives. God calls men and women to the ministry, but one must know that there are callings to pastor a thousand, ten thousand, and there are pastors for fifty or a hundred souls.

In the most beautiful ministry on Earth, all the sick were healed. The preacher who led the ministry would leave a city to go preach in another, and the whole city would go after Him. Not just the dwellers of one particular town—people from all over came to hear Him. He preached to thousands, and thousands got healed. He moved whole cities, delivered the demonized, even raised the dead. But when He ended His public ministry here on Earth, how many souls did He have around Him? Barely one hundred twenty. Do you think this ministry failed?

If we look at it according to our values today, we would have to say that Jesus failed. One hundred twenty souls were in the Upper Room waiting for God's promise. More than five hundred had seen Him after His resurrection, but only one hundred twenty faithful ones were there. Yet, they were the ones to fill the world with Christ, and today we receive the good news as a result of those initial one hundred twenty.

So be aware that maybe God may call you to have a church of a thousand, five hundred, fifty, or twenty. Who cares how many? The important thing is to fulfill God's purpose and plan for our lives.

Beware of triumphalism; we try to achieve success in many ways. We can expect God's blessings, but most of all we need to do His will. That's why so many ministries end in failure—they fail to do *His* will. That's why many ministries, even though they have churches of two and three hundred members, are unhappy and embittered because "it's not enough." If two hundred members is God's will for you, accept it and don't worry about quantities.

God wants people to get saved, but in His way. Not everybody is called to preach in the main cities of the world. Maybe God will send you to a little town, to those difficult places where it's hard to get the people to understand the good news. All souls have value for God. Even those who are not called to pastor have an important part in the kingdom of God. We are part of an army, and the one in the battle zone is not only the courageous one in the forefront but also the one in administration, he who prepares the meals, those who are in charge of helping the warriors. All ministries are important. Yours is too.

3. Knowledge

It's fundamental to possess knowledge, but we should use it to serve the Lord and not to show the world how much we know. It is essential to be trained to answer adequately when we are asked about certain issues. We should understand the Word of God and know how to apply its principles to life situations. Those in ministry should be able to give the right answers because we know our Bible well. If we don't, the devil will have an upper hand since he knows God's Word very well.

God trains us also to minister the love and the grace of Christ through our lives. If all we have is knowledge but no love for lost souls, we won't be able to reach our goal. Everything needs to be well organized and well balanced in order for the ministry to be effective. We need to be able to handle the Word of truth as approved workers, not altering or misusing the truth of the Scriptures.

4. Faith

Faith without works is dead. We may have faith, but if we don't put it into practice, it's useless. If we follow every one of these seven steps but have no faith, there won't be any anointing. To reach the anointing, every single ingredient is necessary.

The Lord tells us clearly, "And these signs will accompany those who believe" (Mark 16:17). He mentions several expressions of power such as healing the sick, casting out demons, and others. Do you believe these signs will accompany you? Who are these signs for? They are meant for all of us—without exception. The Lord tells us today, "Go into all the world and preach the good news to all creation." He will confirm this commission with signs that are activated only by faith.

When you stand behind the pulpit, you put into practice the Word by faith for the purpose of confirming it. God is in charge of the rest. Maybe you wonder what I do. I simply preach the good news as the Bible says in the Gospel of Mark: *I speak the Word.* Once the people have accepted Jesus and come forward to the platform as a public demonstration of their step of faith, I cast out the demons in the name of Jesus Christ, and they come out. I pray for the sick, and they get healed. I also pray, in every meeting, for the baptism of the Holy Spirit. It's very important to fulfill these four facets. Don't neglect to do it, since each one is necessary: salvation, deliverance, healing, and the baptism of the Holy Spirit.

So then, what happens when we pray with faith? The supernatural begins. God's move gets activated by only one key, and that is faith. We need to believe that what we asked for will happen. God never fails.

Some time ago, a pastor invited me to preach at his church. I told him, "Yes, I will come. God has given me something new, and I want to share it." That day, the service was in an uproar. We had all those who wanted the baptism of the Holy Spirit stand in one line, and I started to pray. Every single one I laid my hands on started to speak in tongues. I believed this would happen—and it did. That is faith.

With simplicity, put faith in action. If we truly believe in the Word, God will revolutionize our lives. I try to preach the gospel in the simplest way possible for all to be able to understand. During an evangelistic crusade in the United States, God told me, "Preach one hour, if necessary. The people need to understand that they are the ones who need Me, not I who need them." That is a reality. People need God, so we need to expose their needs by saying, "You need God. Do you plan to continue having a broken heart, drinking, committing adultery, and lying, or do you want to change? Realize that when we turn our backs on God, we choose a life full of pain, sadness, and bitterness."

The gospel is as simple as that. Let's learn the simple things and preach a simple Jesus so everybody can understand God's truths.

5. Action

To understand this step, let's take a look at Nehemiah. He received a word from God telling him to do something. He didn't sit back waiting for God to do it; instead, he went into action and said, "Give your servant success today by granting him favor in the presence of this man" (Neh. 1:11).

Many pray and pray, and when we tell them, "Brother, let's take that neighborhood for Christ," they answer, "We are praying about it." A year later we tell them again, "Brother, we have to take that neighborhood for Christ; there are many drug addicts there." Again their answer is the same—they are praying about it. They spend their lives doing just that, praying. We need to pray, but once God gives us His confirmation we need to stand up as Nehemiah did and say, "Come, let us rebuild the wall of Jerusalem, and we will no longer be in disgrace" (Neh. 2:17). We are always expecting God to do everything; we want Him to come and do the preaching. We pray for two minutes, and then we say, "Lord, save the neighborhood," and that's it. And that is how we expect people to come to the Lord.

Once God gave me a vision of a big oasis with exotic plants, all kinds of fruit trees, streams of crystal clear waters, flowers, dark green grass, birds, and a large crowd drinking refreshing drinks, eating fruit, singing, laughing, and playing. I thought, "This place must be paradise." But as I came closer to the fence around its borders, I saw a desert on the other side. There were no trees, no water, no flowers, and no shade; the hot sun was splitting the rocks in two, and I saw an agonizing crowd staring at us. Many had parched, broken skin; their tongues were swollen, and they had to help each other stand. Their hands were extended toward those of us in paradise, begging for help.

This vision helped me to reflect the church of Jesus. The walls in our buildings are tired of listening to us. Every single brick could become a doctor in theology. Let's take the message of the pulpit to the streets, to the town squares, to the parks. Let's go door-to-door talking about Christ. The cries of those who suffer resonate in our ears. Let's wake up; the news on radio and television, the daily newspapers, and the weekly magazines are singing praise to the destroyer. Let's preach about Jesus Christ!

God wants men and women of action. Let's be sensible and wise. In life, if we don't give ourselves to action, things don't happen. If we don't make an effort, we fail. If there is no action, even when we have great wisdom, we won't win souls for Christ. Even if they build a whole church for us with everything we need in it, forget it! There needs to be action in every one of our projects, and that means going out to serve the Lord.

If you are lazy, just give up your ministry or ask the Lord to remove your laziness. No lazy person can succeed in serving the Lord, because He needs courageous and hard-working people to work for Him. God told Joshua: "Have I not commanded you? Be strong and courageous. Do not be terrified; do not be discouraged" (Josh. 1:9).

What does it mean to work hard? It is to go beyond our limitations. If, for example, we like to sleep a lot, the ministry will not prosper. Everything needs to have a limit and a measure. It isn't necessary, however, to then go to the other extreme and be so busy that all we do is run all day and not pray.

6. Prayer and fasting

We are God's priests. We are responsible for keeping the fires on the altars of our devotional lives burning through constant prayer. Then the fire of the Holy Spirit will never go out.

> The fire on the altar must be kept burning; it must not go out. Every morning the priest is to add firewood and arrange the burnt offering on the fire and burn the fat of the fellowship offerings on it.
> —LEVITICUS 6:12

It is important for us to love lost souls, to bend our knees, to groan and cry out for this lost world. When we accept Jesus, the flames on the altar reach the ceiling. However, with time, the love dies down, and the fire on the altar does too. Then, where there was fire, only ashes remain. If we allow the fire on the altar to go out, as happened to the Levites, we aren't suitable as priests; we fail in our duties. If we don't keep the fire on the altar of God burning in our lives, we will go cold.

We will lose the love we had for souls lost without Christ and cease to care for the work of God and our brothers and sisters.

But, like the church in Ephesus, we can still recover our first love. They forsook their first love and the altar was consumed. They had worked very hard, done much, endured much, but something was wrong. God saw the many efforts of the church in Ephesus, their tireless work. He knew that they didn't tolerate wicked men and that they had tested those who claimed to be apostles and were not. However, He told them, "Yet I hold this against you: You have forsaken your first love. Remember the height from which you have fallen! Repent and do the things you did at first" (Rev. 2:4–5).

We can keep the fire burning with prayer and fasting, seeking God with all our hearts and interceding for the lost. Then we will be prepared to face obstacles, since, as God tells us, "Our struggle is not against flesh and blood, but against the rulers, against the authorities, against the powers of this dark world and against the spiritual forces of evil in the heavenly realms" (Eph. 6:12). The Bible clearly shows us that our struggle is not against men but against the ruler of the kingdom of the air. It is there where we need to have victory, as with unceasing prayer we say, "Satan, let go of the city. Devil, let go of the finances. Satan, filthy devil, you who brings sin over the church, let it go in the name of Jesus Christ."

Satan is real, but many times it seems that we ignore him, believing that he will not hurt us. The devil prowls around like a roaring lion, looking for someone to devour (1 Pet. 5:8). We need to fight this battle in prayer at the altar, and then, every time we rebuke him, it's like throwing gasoline at the fire on the altar.

The consecration, the vision, the knowledge, the faith, and the action are all very important, but we need to give special attention to prayer and fasting. This ingredient cannot be absent from our ministry. If we fail in this, everything else will fail. We need to be careful in all that we do, but it is very important that we always add prayer and intercession. If you are a leader, it is important to organize a group of people who are praying constantly for you, interceding for your life.

7. Love

We have to surround all that we have mentioned until this point with love. If there is no love for lost souls and for our own sheep, the

Christian ministry will be inefficient and will have no fruit in our lives. You may be active and have faith or knowledge, but if you have no love, what good is it? No matter what you build, you will end up destroying it because of your lack of love.

I pray daily: "Lord, give me love. If I don't have love, I'm nothing." If I don't really love those who suffer, I can't continue in the ministry. There are days when I have three people whispering in one ear, three in the other, and three from behind. I can assure you that it isn't always easy, and that is why we need a share of special love. Many times our patience will run dry, and if we don't have any love, we will not be able to go on.

"Love," says the Bible, "...is not proud...it is not self-seeking, it is not easily angered, it keeps no record of wrongs....It always protects, always trusts, always hopes, always perseveres" (1 Cor. 13:4–5, 7). That's the kind of love we are supposed to have. If the fire on your altar is burning, ask God to fill you with His love, and He will do it. But don't forget: pray to God and intercede before Him. Don't be satisfied with praying for five or ten minutes only; it's not enough. Pray to God as much as you want—one hour, two hours—but devote time to the altar. Then all the steps we take in order to have a successful ministry will be flooded with the precious love of our Lord Jesus Christ.

Several years ago, a German pastor sent a brother to us who had written many books. He was investigating everything about revivals and their flaws. He spoke about Finney, Moody, Wesley, and others. He wanted to find out why revivals stop.

I answered him with an illustration. If there are two boxers in a ring, one attacks and the other defends himself. When the one attacking stops, the one defending himself will start to attack. The same happens with the church in her struggle with Satan. When we are fighting for lost souls, what carries the battle on is our love for those lives. When the church stops, the devil attacks. Now the church is on the defensive. Don't ever lose your place of victory within the struggle!

I want to close this chapter with some words that God spoke to me: *Love for the lost produces revival.* When love ceases, revival does too. He who has a passion for souls lives in an ongoing revival.

Chapter 3

AUTHORITY
THROUGH FAITH

SUPERNATURAL SIGNS WILL FOLLOW THOSE WHO RESPOND TO God's calling—God promises that. It's important, however, to remember that each sign is exercised through authority, which in turn receives its boost from faith. God bestows upon Christians a spiritual authority that we need to put into action. Since the Creation, God delegated authority over the earth to men and positioned him as the crown of all creation. The Book of Genesis tells us that God created male and female in His own image. He ordered them to be fruitful and to increase in numbers, telling them to subdue the earth and to rule over the fish of the sea and the birds of the air and over every living creature that moves on the ground (Gen. 1:27–28).

The word *subdue* means "to bring into subjection, under control, to conquer by force or by superior power." Now, the word *rule* means "to control or direct, to exercise authority or power over, to play a dominant role in or exert a controlling influence over, and to hold preeminence in (as by ability, strength, or position)." From these definitions we can interpret these words to express power; they delineate the real dominance and authority over every living creature that was given by God to man.

But that rule was lost when man sinned. Satan took away man's authority and became the ruler of the earth. Man lost the title deed to his authority when Satan snatched it out of his hands.

And yet, when Jesus died on the cross, He not only redeemed us, but He also removed the barrier that separated us from Him, giving us the possibility of becoming children of God. In so doing, He took authority away from the devil and automatically put it back into our hands. I guarantee you that we have authority proceeding from God, and through faith in Him we can take anything away from the devil. Just believe that we are the real heirs and coheirs with Christ in the kingdom of heaven. Our Father is the owner. He has the title deed to this earth.

When we assume our rights by faith, we are equipped to exercise authority over all the demonic powers of this world. If Satan is controlling a person or situation, we have the power to cast him out since we have recovered all divine authority through the power of the cross of Jesus Christ.

A clear example of this can be seen in what happened to us in Argentina when we began our crusades. At that time, we were not allowed to preach the gospel of Jesus Christ on the radio or television. In 1992, when we, together with eighty local churches, held a big crusade in a northern province, we asked several radio and television stations to sell us airtime so we could broadcast our services live. They wanted a lot of money for this service, since a few days before in that same city there had been an important political function and the radio stations had been able to get as much money as they wanted.

We also had problems with the site we had chosen for setting up our tent. The authorities did not want to give us the plot of land, even though they had lent it to circuses and to anybody who would request it for other purposes than ours. But that didn't stop us either. God was continuing to work in the situation. A brother gave us a field he owned in the outskirts of the city. The only inconvenience was the lack of transportation to that site. There was only one occasional bus, and that worried us—how were the people going to come to the crusade every night?

The days prior to the crusade were difficult ones. The team was discouraged. We decided to declare spiritual warfare, and we rebuked the devil, saying, "Satan, move back. We bind you in the name of Jesus. Let go of the means of communication. Go away, strongman; you are defeated."

We prayed for several days. When the meetings began, we could feel strong support coming from God. During one of our times of intercession for the crusade, the Holy Spirit gave visions to different brothers of the strongman falling from his throne together with demonic structures.

One morning, God told me, "You have to transmit this crusade simultaneously by radio and television." I knew that God was giving radio and television time to us; the strongman was defeated. I spoke with our team coordinator, Brother Tito Meda, and told him to buy the radio and television airtime that was needed.

There the surprise began. The media executives accepted our proposal to pay only 30 percent of the value they had proposed at the beginning. The FM radio station broadcast the crusade at no cost. On Saturday, more than ten different radio and television stations broadcast the service.

But there was more. One evening, five minutes after the beginning of the broadcast, the television channels we had not contracted had a technical problem and had to discontinue their regular programs. The only thing the entire city could watch that night was our crusade. Our Lord is wonderful!

We saw many people run to the platform to meet with God that night. Four young men arrived at the place by car. They were in such a state of desperation that before they had heard the preaching on the radio, they had decided to commit suicide in the car. Thousands more came. There were hundreds of incredible miracles happening. One of them was really awesome. A mother put her little child with Down syndrome in front of the television screen. As I was praying, she saw her son being healed and his facial features changing right before her eyes. Hundreds of teeth were filled with gold and platinum fillings, and several cancer patients got healed.

After that first broadcast, the crusade took off. Nobody could understand how we got so much airtime with so little money. But we knew why. Through faith, we had taken hold of God's authority. As a result, the entire city was shaken under Jesus's power. We preached for thirty-eight days in that place, and more than thirty thousand people accepted Jesus for the glory and honor of our Lord.

A pastor from the province of Jujuy had a doctor at his church who would buy him an airplane ticket to Buenos Aires every month so that he could attend classes at the Bible seminary. On the plane, whenever the flight attendant would ask him if he wanted a soft drink, because he had no money he would always respond, "No, thanks." After many trips, he finally graduated from seminary. As an award for his achievements, he received some money. That day, as he got on the plane for his return home, he was anxiously waiting for the flight attendant to offer him something to eat or drink. This time he accepted her offering. Right before the landing, the pastor called the flight attendant and asked her how much he owed her for the exquisite food and drinks she had brought him. She, with a big smile, said, "Nothing, of course. Everything is included in the airfare."

The pastor was astonished! He had never been able to enjoy anything because he didn't know it was free.

The same happens with the church of Jesus Christ. Because of our ignorance, we do not enjoy the benefits that God offers His children.

READY TO UNDERSTAND

In a vision, a man dressed in linen told Daniel not to be afraid, that since the first day he had set his mind to gain understanding and to humble himself before his God, his words had been heard. But something happened to this man as he was carrying God's answer to Daniel. He encountered resistance, and for twenty-one days a fierce spiritual battle was fought in the air (Dan. 10:12–13).

What the angel meant when he used the words "to gain understanding" is that faith can also be interpreted. When I read the Bible, I analyze what it teaches me through faith, even when my ideas and prejudices come in between and try to limit it. This happens to many people. People with scientific knowledge, for example, possess ideas that are difficult to dismantle when the time comes to accept things by faith. In churches, some preconceived ideas simply stop the growth of the church. Only the Holy Spirit can, in a supernatural way, tear down those ideas and prejudices.

When we don't possess these kinds of preconceived ideas, we have easier access to the spiritual realm. A clear example is the simple faith of children. Jesus said that unless we become like children, we will never enter the kingdom of heaven (Matt. 18:3). Children accept and believe with total innocence. They don't have preconceived ideas. On the contrary, they receive and accept by faith whatever their parents or elders tell them. In the Book of Luke we read that Jesus rejoiced over the fact that His Father had hidden the things of the Spirit from the wise and learned and revealed them to little children (Luke 10:21).

Although many try to understand God through their intellects, we can only know Him by faith. We will find people who will say the things of God are pure "madness" and those who believe the good news are "fools." God saves us by faith and not because of our understanding. Let's be like children in the way we believe.

Don't Limit Your Faith

Some say that there is a supercomputer that contains all the knowledge available to man. Its memory is filled with incredible data provided by the scientists and is capable of providing all kinds of information in every area of human knowledge. I imagine it could even provide secret information about any country in the world. But if we would ask the computer to give us information on some spiritual issue, it would not be able to, because it doesn't understand the supernatural.

Man possesses a spirit that enables him to have access, through faith, to all levels of life, even to the spiritual level. In a sense, we could say that we are supernatural because we have a spirit in us that is capable of interpreting spiritual things. In Galatians 5:22–23, the Bible lists the graces that constitute the fruit of the Spirit: love, joy, peace, patience, kindness, goodness, faithfulness, gentleness, and self-control. We can clearly see that faith is a fruit of the Spirit and that only man has access to it because he is the only living creature that possesses a spirit. Only through faith can we interpret the things of the Spirit and have access to God's authority. We are also able to distinguish two types of faith: the *natural* and the *supernatural.*

One summer night during my first mission trip to the north of Argentina, I was asked to preach for the reopening of a church. We invited people to the three-day crusade. We prepared benches made out of old pieces of wood and tree trunks. On the first day, only a few came, but as they witnessed God's power, they ran to tell their friends about the signs and wonders that were taking place. On the second day, many more came; on the last, the church was full.

I was moved when I realized that most of them didn't know the Lord. It had been worth traveling over one thousand kilometers to get there. At the first meeting, shortly after we had started, I saw the people become agitated. Some were scratching themselves, others were waving their arms, and some of the children were very restless. A swarm of mosquitoes had come into the building, and the mosquitoes were afflicting those present. They sprayed the place with repellent, but the mosquitoes seemed to multiply. Our natural faith was not working. Imagine how difficult this was for me. As the preacher, I was convinced that when I started to preach, the people were going to be totally distracted by the mosquitoes and would pay no attention to my words.

At that moment, God told me to throw the mosquitoes out of the church. Here is where the supernatural faith was going to start working. But I said, "Lord, how do You expect me to do that? If I throw them out and they don't go, I will be the one who will have to go." But since He insisted, I responded, "All right, if You give me the faith to do it, I will throw them out." This is the eternal struggle between natural faith, which tells our minds that something is impossible, and God's faith, which says, "Do it now."

When the pastor introduced me to the congregation, I stood up. Suddenly a supernatural faith came over me. Like David face-to-face with Goliath, I had no doubts about the victory. I said, "Brothers and sisters, stand up and let us pray and cast these mosquitoes out in the name of Jesus. Now! Right now!" In seconds all the mosquitoes were gone. A gentle breeze drove them out of God's house. The people were in awe, and God's name was glorified.

When I analyzed what had happened, I understood that when God gave Adam authority over all the living creatures, that included mosquitoes. I was the one with the problem. I did not have supernatural faith to believe that the mosquitoes would leave at my rebuke. I had difficulty doing what I needed to do since my natural faith was telling me I was crazy and had no power to do it. Those were just prejudices, preconceived ideas. I took the risk, however, to believe by faith and assumed divine authority. And supernatural faith gave me the authority to do it!

Prejudices form such solid structures in the human being that they don't allow faith to develop with authority. I'm not only talking about those who don't believe in Jesus or who have no faith to believe in Him. I'm also talking about those who believe but who limit their supernatural faith. The Bible tells us about the time when Philip met Jesus. He was so thrilled that he ran to tell his friend Nathanael. He told him he had found Jesus, Joseph's son, the carpenter from Nazareth. Nathanael's reaction was, "Nazareth! Can anything good come from there?" (John 1:45–46).

From this we realize that the city of Nazareth didn't have a good reputation, and this fact consequently affected Jesus. Probably Nathanael wouldn't have approached Jesus if it hadn't been for Philip's insistence. His prejudices could have stopped him from meeting Jesus and being saved. Only when Nathanael approached Jesus, who revealed His power to him, were the structures limiting his faith broken.

Even religion can be God's enemy. It may generate restraining prejudices and preconceived religious ideas. People don't believe in miracles until they experience them in their own lives or in the lives of their loved ones. That's why they need signs and wonders to have faith in God.

WHEREVER THE PRESENCE OF GOD IS, THERE WILL BE SIGNS

I know that wherever God is present, there will be signs. We need to tear down all prejudices that limit our access to supernatural faith and assume by faith the authority handed down to us by God. Signs break down the preexisting structures. Through them many have access to a life of faith. The Bible teaches us that signs will accompany those who believe.

> And these signs will accompany those who believe: In my name they will drive out demons; they will speak in new tongues; they will pick up snakes with their hands; and when they drink deadly poison, it will not hurt them at all; they will place their hands on sick people, and they will get well.
>
> —MARK 16:17–18

I firmly believe that these signs are not for the church but for the unbelievers. I think God gives signs throughout His church so that others may believe. I can personally perceive this in my crusades. People believe, and then their faith gets activated when they see God's signs: the cripple walking, cancer getting healed, somebody who was oppressed being delivered from demons. That's the reason why in every meeting I invite the people who have received their miracle to come up to the platform to share and testify about their experience. This encourages people to believe, and it challenges their faith.

When God sent Moses to lead Israel out of Egypt, Moses told Him that the people were not going to believe Jehovah had really spoken to him. So God showed him a staff, and then He changed it into a snake. Moses got scared and ran from it. But God told him to extend his hand and take the snake by the tail. As he did this, the snake became a staff again in his hand. This and other signs would show the people of Israel that God had truly been with him. (See Exodus 4:2–9.)

So the people of Israel also needed signs to believe. As they saw them, even unbelievers believed and followed Moses. God had endorsed and inspired these signs to cause the people to believe. Even though they didn't see God, they knew that He was behind the signs.

It was the same thing with Nicodemus; when he approached Jesus he said, "Rabbi, we know you are a teacher who has come from God. For no one could perform the miraculous signs you are doing if God were not with him" (John 3:2). This man recognized, through the miraculous signs of Jesus, that God endorsed him. Jesus's public ministry was full of signs, and large crowds followed Him just to see His power to heal and deliver.

When John the Baptist doubted, what did Jesus do? Let's read in the Bible the account of what happened:

> John's disciples told him about all these things. Calling two of them, he sent them to the Lord to ask, "Are you the one who was to come, or should we expect someone else?"
>
> When the men came to Jesus, they said, "John the Baptist sent us to you to ask, 'Are you the one who was to come, or should we expect someone else?'"
>
> At that very time Jesus cured many who had diseases, sicknesses and evil spirits, and gave sight to many who were blind. So he

replied to the messengers, "Go back and report to John what you have seen and heard: The blind receive sight, the lame walk, those who have leprosy are cured, the deaf hear, the dead are raised, and the good news is preached to the poor."

—LUKE 7:18–22

Jesus didn't tell them, "Don't you realize with what wisdom I speak to you?" Jesus showed them signs. In this way, John was going to be able to recognize who He was. God always communicated with His children through signs. For example, He led His people through the desert with a pillar of cloud by day and a pillar of fire by night. That was a sign. The manna that fell from heaven every morning was another sign. Gideon's fleece was another. And Jesus's healing the sick was a sign also. There is a whole world of people out there who are searching for the true way. God wants them to know that Jesus is the way; the signs are but a demonstration of His presence with us.

THE TRUE CHURCH

When we study the tabernacle of Israel, we observe several elements that reveal great truths about God to us. But there is an element in particular that I want to focus on—the ark of the covenant.

The tabernacle was divided into several different areas. One area was the most holy place, the place where the presence of God dwelt and to which only the high priest had access once a year, and only then after going through several previous rituals. The ark of the covenant rested there. In it were the tablets of the Law and Aaron's staff. I could mention several things about this, but I want you to realize that where God's presence is there are signs. And this staff represented God's signs.

The world is looking for signs to find the correct way. God gave signs to us, as He did to Moses, to John the Baptist, and to Nicodemus. But many sects, religions, warlocks, witches, magicians, psychics, and enlightened ones stand up with false signs, claiming to be the incarnation of Jesus or saying, "This is the way." So, what should we do with such lies and deceptions from the devil? Are we going to proclaim the gospel with wise and persuasive words, or are we going to do it with a demonstration of the power of the Holy Spirit?

If you want to identify the true church, look for the signs of God described in the following passage:

> Go into all the world and preach the good news to all creation. Whoever believes and is baptized will be saved, but whoever does not believe will be condemned. And these signs will accompany those who believe: In my name they will drive out demons; they will speak in new tongues; they will pick up snakes with their hands; and when they drink deadly poison, it will not hurt them at all; they will place their hands on sick people, and they will get well.
>
> —MARK 16:15–18

The first part—"preach the good news to all creation"—may be common to many churches, because they preach the gospel. Others baptize those who believe. But that which distinguishes the true church are the signs that will accompany those who believe. Therefore, look for a church where the signs promised by God are present, where the spiritually oppressed find deliverance, where heavenly tongues are spoken, where there are confrontations with evil, and where the sick get well.

Our Lord Jesus Christ gave all authority to His disciples for them to go and heal the sick and deliver the demonized. The Bible says:

> He called his twelve disciples to him and gave them authority to drive out evil spirits and to heal every disease and sickness.
>
> —MATTHEW 10:1

God gave you and me that same authority. With it we can show the world the signs of God so they will believe. Christ Himself amazed people because of His authority, and the religious people of His time asked Him, "What is this? A new teaching—and with authority! He even gives orders to evil spirits and they obey him" (Mark 1:27). For the religious structures and their strongly established prejudices, Christ's authority was a new doctrine. Today that authority is yours and mine.

Accept the challenge of assuming God's authority by faith to confront sicknesses, demons, and every spiritual barrier that can only be overcome by faith. We are heirs of one of the biggest fortunes there is, and yet we don't use it.

Take authority by faith, and you will obtain unbelievable results.

Part Three

"THEY WILL DRIVE OUT DEMONS..."

Chapter 4

DEMONOLOGY 101

A REALITY WE FACE EVERY DAY IS ENCOUNTERING PEOPLE with demonic powers. This is nothing new for those who read the Bible. In it we read about people who were delivered from demons. The following story is an example of the kind of demonic power we encounter in our ministry:

"SATAN HAD ME BOUND"

For forty-two years, I suffered from depression. Even as a little girl it isolated me from other children; I didn't want to play with them. I remember always climbing up a tree in our back yard. There I could hide from the rest of the world.

I have five sisters, but none were like me. They were always laughing. Many times people would tell my mom, "How well behaved this little girl is!" What they didn't know is that the reason I was so quiet was I was terrified inside. I didn't know how to play; I didn't know how to laugh.

My entire life was impacted by what I had to go through as a child, and it had to do with my father, who was an alcoholic. He used to beat my mother and my sisters, always carrying weapons and constantly threatening us, saying that he was going to kill us while we slept. Because of this, every night I would try to stay awake until I was overcome by sleep. I was terrified and had terrible nightmares. I would wake up and see the shadow of a man opening my closet door and putting on my father's coat and hat.

Whenever I was afraid I would run to my backyard and sit for hours by a pear tree. Since my family didn't know what was the matter with me, they could not help me.

The bad relationship between my dad and my mom and us had consequences for the rest of my life. Because of it, I didn't want to get married. Perhaps I tied myself down—not wanting to go through the same thing that my mother had to go through.

The depression continued throughout my youth and adult life. I lived constantly locked in my room in complete darkness. I smoked all day, drank, and played the game of the cup. I also had a strong inclination for the occult. I liked it. I was always trying to move objects with the power of my mind, and I used to read palms. I also read tarot cards, predicting the future of those who asked. All these demonic bondages drove me to an even deeper pit of desolation.

One day my mother told me about some meetings taking place in the city of Moreno. It was one of Brother Annacondia's crusades. Right away I felt I needed to go. During those days a very loud voice started to tell me to drink poison and kill myself to bring my misery to an end. But I was so sick that I didn't have the strength to go out and buy the poison.

The crusade lasted fifty-two days, but I only got there four days before it was finished. All that time, the devil wouldn't stop compelling me to commit suicide. One afternoon my mother invited me to go out. We got on a bus that passed right in front of the tent where the crusade was held. I started to scream, saying I wanted to get off. I was loud; all the passengers were staring at me, and the driver simply had to stop to let us off. When I got off, I ran into the tent where the crusade was taking place.

On February 12, 1987, I accepted Jesus into my heart. That first night I didn't want to leave that place. I was so happy; my life had changed, and the depression had left. During the following meetings, something inside didn't allow me to go up front so that Brother Annacondia could pray for me. But the last night of the crusade, I finally did. When they started to pray for me, I started to shake uncontrollably. The counselors took me to the tent of deliverance, and there they continued to pray for me. I had to renounce many things that were in my heart, including hatred and bitterness. The devil had me in such bondage that I was in complete torment. When I decided in my heart to be free, however, the Lord brought change right away.

Several times I had to renounce certain things before God that had been hidden in my heart. In one of those times, as I was praying with others, some felt from God that I had a spirit of divination and that I had been involved with tarot cards. So they started to rebuke that evil spirit and to pray for my deliverance. Suddenly, we heard a loud noise, like a cup exploding, and I was completely delivered.

Soon after, my family also came to the Lord. They saw the change God produced in me. The neighbors started to see me walking out in the street during the day and wondered what had happened. I had always been in my room, sleeping all day, and by the time I woke up it was already dark outside. So I lived in darkness. The time would go by, and I would complain for not having done anything all day. That's why all the people who knew me could see the change in me. Now I get up early, I smile, and I go to church. God truly changed my life.

—MARÍA

Christians either underestimate or overestimate Satan. But God teaches us exactly where to stand before the forces of evil. We know very well that Satan is like a roaring lion, roaming the earth and looking for someone to devour. This we know. We also know that "these signs will accompany those who believe: In my name they will drive out demons" (Mark 16:17). Therefore, don't be afraid. If you believe in the Lord Jesus Christ and obey His command to "go and preach," these are the signs that you will encounter in your journey.

Demons are evil beings that have no material bodies, and they go around looking for a place in which to dwell. They speak, they reason, they see, and they hear. There are many examples of this; the Book of Mark gives us a few. When Jesus was preaching in the synagogue, those present were amazed at His teaching because He taught as one who had authority. They had not perceived the same authority in others, not even in the teachers of the Law. But something happened. A man inside the synagogue started to scream. Right away, Jesus recognized that an evil spirit was speaking through this man's mouth, saying, "What do you want with us, Jesus of Nazareth? Have you come to destroy us? I know who you are—the Holy One of God!" But Jesus rebuked him sternly, saying, "Be quiet!…Come out of him!" (Mark 1:24–25).

Now let's examine this unusual situation in the synagogue. This happened at the time of Jesus's teaching, not before. The individual who was possessed was inside the place. And it is interesting to notice that although the religious men admired Jesus and His teachings, they didn't recognize Him as the Messiah—yet the demons did.

Only with our spirit can we recognize the spiritual world. This is what happened when Jesus heard the man screaming. Immediately He told him to be quiet and to come out of that body. The demons struggled to stay; they shook the man violently, and they finally came out with a shriek. After this, the people started to recognize that Jesus had spiritual authority, and they asked each other, "What is this teaching? With authority and power he gives orders to evil spirits and they come out!" (Luke 4:36).

DEMONIC MANIFESTATIONS

There are many different demonic manifestations in people. They look different in different people.

The oppressed

It is common to see people spiritually oppressed. The oppression works on the outside; it never ceases, and its only purpose is to break down our resistance. It manifests itself through temptations and persecutions. It's usually Christians who suffer this type of oppression. It's the devil's way of trying to get people to go back to their old sinful lives. That's why the Bible tells us not to give the devil a foothold but to resist him.

The tormented

Demons torment people. In this type of manifestation, the evil spirit is inside the person and works from within. There are fear, depression, and affliction. But let us be clear in this: a tormented person who manifests a spiritual problem isn't necessarily demonized. There aren't that many demonized people in the world, but there are many tormented by the devil. The person doesn't offer any resistance, but the demons are there; we simply have to cast and drive them out as we are told to do in Mark 16:17. We drive them out in the name of Jesus.

Let's consider the example of the Syrophoenician woman who told Jesus, "My daughter is suffering terribly from demon-possession" (Matt. 15:22).

After a brief conversation, Jesus told her, "You may go; the demon has left your daughter" (Mark 7:29). If the demon "*left* your daughter," it's because the demon *was inside*. If not, Jesus probably would have said, "He has left your daughter's side."

The tormented person is not demonized. There is an area of his or her life that is under the devil's influence either because he or she has not given it to the Lord or because there is a pact or a bondage, maybe hatred or resentment. We all know very well that when these feelings are buried down deep in our hearts, a door opens for the devil to come into our lives and create havoc. This is very real and not a mere invention.

The possessed

People who are possessed temporarily lose the ability to control their bodies and will. After being delivered and counseled, they don't remember what they went through right before the deliverance. The demonized lose control of their actions. They do things that they don't remember afterward. Suddenly they get enraged and break and burn objects. When they come back to their senses, if questioned, they will say they don't remember anything at all.

Let's take a look at the father who took his son to Jesus to be delivered from a spirit that had robbed him of speech. The father tells Jesus that at times the spirit would seize the boy and throw him on the ground. The boy would foam at the mouth, gnash his teeth, and become rigid. He also added that often the spirit had thrown the boy into the water or into the fire, trying unsuccessfully to kill him. I really think this father had a lot of faith; how clearly he described his son's suffering and with what spiritual maturity he interpreted that it was an evil spirit that had possessed his son. The father also said that this had been happening from childhood. He was also right in declaring that it was a mute spirit. His son didn't speak, didn't scream. He had described many different ways in which the boy had been forced by the demon to manifest externally, but screaming was not one of them.

Let us see now how Jesus delivered this young boy. He said, "You deaf and mute spirit...I command you, come out of him and never enter him again" (Mark 9:25). The first thing Jesus did was call him out; He said: "Listen to me, you deaf and mute spirit." But if he was deaf, how could he hear? Brothers and sisters, never forget that Satan is the father of lies and a deceiver. Take a look at what happened after Jesus rebuked him: "The spirit shrieked, convulsed him violently and came out. The boy looked so much like a corpse that many said, 'He's dead'" (v. 26). Now all of a sudden the demon was screaming and shouting. So, do you still believe him? Jesus knew with whom He was dealing. He can't be deceived.

The insane

Lastly, this type of manifestation indicates a complete and permanent possession. The devil has taken possession of the body, the soul, and the spirit. It's the total opposite of the person filled by the Holy Spirit. This was the case of the Gadarene man. He was completely isolated from others and had a violent behavior. He would hurt himself, cutting himself with stones. I have seen insane people in mental hospitals. They look but don't see. If you talk to them, you are not sure they're listening. They don't understand anything because they're totally dominated by evil spirits. Maybe you wonder if it is possible for them to be delivered. God has compassion for them also. Just as He delivered the Gadarene, He can deliver others too.

THE GADARENE FROM THE CITY OF CÓRDOBA

The last evening of a sixty-day crusade in the city of Córdoba in Argentina was coming to an end. As I was descending from the platform, ready to go back to my hotel, some brothers stopped me and asked me if I could pray for a madman. This man was really crazy; he was like the Gadarene demoniac. He lived in the mountains, he would speak to himself, he was half-naked and barefoot, his hair was incredibly dirty (he hadn't taken a bath in three years), and he had long nails. He truly looked like an animal. That last night I was feeling really tired after such a long crusade, and right when I was ready to go, they brought to me this man so I could pray for him. Four stretcher-bearers were carrying him.

As I was coming closer, the Holy Spirit said to me, "There are two legions."

To this I answered, "Lord, I have no strength left and my voice is failing." But I still laid my hands on him and rebuked every demon, saying, "In the name of Jesus, let go of this body." The man started to run and run until we couldn't see him anymore, so I declared him free by faith.

Six months later, I returned to the city of Córdoba for a special meeting on the Day of Pentecost. Many people gave their testimony, sharing how God had healed and delivered them in our last crusade. Among those people, a very well-dressed man came up to share how God had set him free. At that moment, the leaders of the city told me, "Brother Carlos, do you remember this man?" I had no idea who he was, but as he shared, I was amazed to see the change in him.

I learned that after we had prayed for him six months earlier, the "Gadarene from Córdoba" went running to the middle of a field and just stood there screaming for five whole days. Demons would come out with every cry. On the last day, the man started to walk toward what once had been his home. When his family saw him, they just couldn't understand what had happened since he was totally normal again; he was a changed man. The night I prayed for that man I was very tired, but God doesn't need our efforts or our abilities. He is sovereign over all.

Satan works in people's lives in different ways, and yet all his activity is aimed at stealing, killing, and destroying (John 10:10). Jesus declares that the devil is a murderer from the beginning, that there is no truth in him. He also says that he lies, even lies about himself, since he's not only a liar but also the father of all lies (John 8:44). What can we expect of somebody who is a thief, a murderer, a destroyer, and a liar like him?

FAMILY CURSES

Every time we curse, we are invoking a spirit. Many times, the reason people need deliverance is because others have cursed them, especially parents. One of the most common curses is when grandparents, uncles and aunts, or parents give away their descendants by Satan's request. They just don't know the terrible consequences of doing this. All generational curses produce frustrations and hereditary failures that have to be severed.

The Bible says that there are things bound on the earth that need to be loosed in heaven. That's what we need to do. It is quite common, especially in the Hispanic culture, to create ties through family mandates and judgments. We have received inherited curses even as children. Some examples are: "You are just like your father"; "You will always be dumb"; or "You are no good." The spoken word expresses authority. God spoke the world into existence. The spoken word builds up, and it also tears down. It is a common thing to hear parents or siblings calling a child "crazy" or "dumb." Through these words we invoke demonic spirits and tie the child up. Words have the power to bind.

Some time ago, I severely corrected one of my children when I heard him say something terrible to his brother. I was really troubled when I heard him speak like that. Never allow such words to be spoken in your family! As Christians, our responsibility is to bless, to bring blessing to others even through our words. Whenever I talk to my children, I say, "How are you, genius?" "What are you up to, champion?"

Some mothers are totally unaware of this truth, and so their children, as they grow, pay the consequences of what their mothers pronounced over them. I've known men whose moms have told them, "Why were you ever born? I wonder why I ever brought you into this world!" These young men's lives were impacted until they found Jesus, and finally their wounds were healed.

When we say "idiot" or "moron," we express our momentary anger. We don't realize that there are consequences to pay for this in the spiritual realm. The following young man's testimony clearly reflects Hispanic culture and its use of common negative phrases.

RESCUED FROM GENERATIONAL CURSES

I was born into a family where men and women for many generations had lived as they wanted, certainly always doing things against God's will. I therefore received an inheritance of corruption, sickness, and death. But one who serves the devil as I did is not born like that but becomes that way.

As a child, I was severely punished verbally and physically. My parents would say, "Children need to be punished with harshness." Then they would add, almost like trying to justify themselves, "I only punish you because I love you."

The teachers in school used to tell me, "You are going to do it because I tell you to do it"; "You are going to understand it no matter what"; and "I will straighten you out."

Whenever I did something wrong or mischievous, I was immediately condemned with a terrible prophecy: "You are just like your father." And then they would go on adding other popular sayings that emphasized the fact that I had no hope of ever changing. They called me crow, pig, donkey, good for nothing, lazy, wretched, and other terrible names. Of course, all this was done to correct and teach me!

I had to forgive all this in the name of Jesus in order to stop living in bondage to hatred, fear, and my family's false doctrines.

My elders, whom I venerated, also taught me some other things. They used to say, "Where there is a will there is a way," or "Faith moves mountains" (of course, they weren't talking about faith in God, but in man). They also said, "Never say die" and "You're young; you have the whole world in your hands." They constantly repeated, "The biggest treasure a father can give his son is education and a career so he can succeed in life." Along with this, they said, "If you want to amount to anything, you need to study." If I became a doctor, the whole family was going to reap the rewards. They declared, "If you don't study, you will be a poor wretch." Or they said things like, "You will be what you have to be, or you will be nothing." They stated, "To own things is power"; "Money doesn't make you happy, but it helps"; "When you have a full stomach, you have a happy heart"; "The most important thing in life is to be healthy"; and other phrases like that.

If they ever caught me reading something spiritual or going to the Catholic church too often, they would laugh and say, "That's all we need; now he's becoming a priest!" From the priests, the phrases I remember the most are "Know yourself" and "Take care of yourself, help yourself, and perfect yourself."

There was a whole load of "shoulds" and "oughts" that crushed me...everything was about effort, willpower, sacrifice, suffering, remorse, resignation, and being smart and polite.

They also taught me that one has to assert oneself. And in high school they taught me that man is a rational animal and that "I think, therefore I am." By the time I was twenty years old they had succeeded in convincing me that man is in charge of his own destiny.

The world was, according to my painful experience, selfish, hostile, deceitful, and hypocritical. They told me, however, that the world wasn't like that, that it was only my perception of it, because "the thief believes that everybody is a thief."

They not only taught me false doctrines, but they also instructed me to teach as they did, believing that I was communicating truth. Finally I decided to study clinical and social psychology, parapsychology, Zen Buddhism, astrology, and folk medicine. In this way I became a false teacher—the blind leading the blind.*

In October 1984 I attended, together with a group of psychologists and student friends, a Carlos Annacondia crusade in the city of Lomas de Zamora, Argentina, for the sole purpose of investigating. I really didn't want to go; I was tired of false healings, but my friends took me anyway.

During the crusade, they invited the sick to come up front so they could pray for them. Since I suffered from hereditary and incurable allergies, I went up front to be able to prove the truth of these signs. Suddenly, I found myself crying out to God for salvation and for the love I had never known. I then understood that I had been a suitable instrument in Satan's hands. Blessed be the Lord Jesus Christ who didn't look at my wickedness and the large amount of lives I had pushed over to the abyss, but who rescued me to show me His love!

—Basilio

This story causes us to reflect and think about how many times we have said all those familiar phrases. I imagine that each culture has its own phrases. But we frequently hear those words, especially between those who love each other—spouses, parents, children, brothers, and sisters. Don't allow this to go on in your life. Remove those words from your vocabulary. Realize that some of the failures we experience in life are a consequence of all this. Don't impact the lives of your loved ones by talking this way.

Spiritually, these words have great value. The devil takes advantage of them to make the person who has received the sentence or curse believe it's true. Sooner or later, they will wound the person to such an extent that only the ministry of the Holy Spirit can heal and enable the person to forgive the offenders.

---

* See chapter 8 for a more detailed account of this period in the life of this man.

God teaches us that the tongue has the power of life and death, and those who love it will eat its fruit (Prov. 18:21). Curses bind lives and stop the blessings. Learn how to bless your children, your spouse, and your parents, and you will notice a big change.

The apostle Peter teaches, "For, 'Whoever would love life and see good days must keep his tongue from evil and his lips from deceitful speech'" (1 Pet. 3:10). Our tongues cause a lot of pain; only Christ can bring healing to the situation, but only if we are willing to recognize our wrongdoing.

If we want a good life, we need to refrain from speaking evil. Spiritual forces of evil participate in these kinds of curses. Satan is not omniscient; he can't read my thoughts, but he does understand what I declare with my mouth. That's why it's so important to confess blessings and not curses. Remember the fig tree that withered when cursed? (See Matthew 21:19.)

Confession is extremely important. When people accept Jesus Christ as Savior and Lord of their lives by faith, I always tell them to repeat their prayers aloud. The devil has to hear them declaring their confession of faith. Many times I see people standing before the platform who, when the call comes for them to offer their lives to Jesus, do not repeat aloud what I am telling them. So I tell them to shout. The devil has to hear them. When some say, "I prayed mentally," I tell them that the devil didn't hear them. The Bible speaks clearly about this in Romans 10:10: "For it is with your heart that you believe and are justified, and it is with your mouth that you confess and are saved."

Sometimes I see people struggling to say, "Lord, here is my life," or "Lord, I receive You in my heart." It is because, at that very moment, there is a spiritual battle taking place in their hearts. There is no room for two kingdoms in our hearts. One has to go, and that depends solely on the will and free choice of the person making this very important decision.

Chapter 5

DEMONOLOGY 102

THE DEVIL'S POWER IS OFTEN EXPRESSED THROUGH occultish expressions of witchcraft and sorcery. We have encountered these powers many times and have seen many people delivered from a lifetime of witchcraft. The woman in the story below is one such example.

"THREE TIMES HE COMMANDED ME TO KILL MYSELF"

I had had mental problems since I was a little girl. It started when I realized I was clairvoyant—I could see what was going to happen; I knew facts, people, places. Somebody was revealing things of the past and the future to me. It always scared me because I had no control over these situations, and they were increasing more and more every day.

My family took me to a psychologist, but nothing could be done. I was so upset with the doctor that once, when I was nine years old, I moved a pencil holder that was on his desk—with my mind. The poor doctor freaked out; he just didn't know what to think or do. He was amazed by my answers because he realized I knew a lot of things. He finally gave up on me and told my mother he couldn't help me.

They took me to see other doctors who performed several tests, including an electroencephalogram, but to no avail. So they decided to take me to a parapsychologist. She told us that it would be detrimental for me to reject the power I had—that I had to accept it. Besides, she said she was going to help me to develop it. After attending several of her classes, I realized that she was using me for her own purposes. I left and started going to three spiritualistic centers. They almost drove me crazy.

In later days, I could see silhouettes in broad daylight. I would hear murmuring, voices calling me. I would see weird shapes. At night I couldn't sleep; I would have nightmares, hear noises of chains and voices commanding me to do things. I felt that somebody was dragging me by the hair, throwing me against the wall. My father was heavily built, but even he couldn't hold me during these episodes because of the strength I would suddenly develop. My mother used to hold my hands so I would not tear my hair out.

Once, in our back yard, I saw a shadow chasing me. When I turned around, I saw a man with dark hair and penetrating black eyes. He looked very serious and was staring at me accusingly. I was paralyzed by fear and started to scream, "Mom, Mom!" When I turned around again, there was my father trying to hold me down while I was jumping and banging all over the place.

Sometime later, things began to quiet down. But at the beginning of 1987, it all came back. I thought that was the end. I tried to kill myself three times, even when I didn't want to do it. Once, I took a knife to bed, and a voice said to me, "Now, do it; it won't hurt. It's the only solution you have left. You are losing your mind." I would see in dreams how my life would evolve if I didn't kill myself. I could see myself in a pit, with hands and feet tied up, long hair, a dirty white tunic, and many people around the pit throwing stuff at me. The voice would say, "This is how it will be."

In February 1988 I went to Brother Annacondia's crusade in the city of Solano. The first night, I ended up in the tent where they prayed for deliverance. I only remember waking up crying and drenched in sweat. During those days I started to feel peace, love, and joy. A new life was beginning.

One night after the crusade, something woke me up. When I opened my eyes, I saw a very strong man in front of me who said, "I am King Thor; you are mine, and you will not leave me." (Thor is a god in Scandinavian mythology that rules over the forces of nature, storms, and war.) I wanted to worship God, but my tongue felt like cement. I made an effort and started to say over and over, "There is power in the blood of Jesus." A crusade counselor had taught me that during one of the meetings. Afterward, I started to worship God with all my heart.

One night, a serpent appeared in one of my dreams. Its head was much bigger than its body. The place was flooded with dirty water up to my knees, and it was raining, much like a big storm. Suddenly, the serpent started to laugh and go around me in circles. I turned to the serpent and said, "I'm not afraid of you." I cast it out in the name of Jesus and it left. It came back three times, and every time I would rebuke it. But the last time it stopped laughing when it heard me say, "Evil spirit, I cast you out in the name of Jesus. Go back to the abyss from where you came." I remember it was so scared, it started to jump.

Today I go to church. When I remember and look back at my past, I realize that all that happened to me was because of my ancestors who offered my life to witchcraft.

—SANDRA

RULERS AND PRINCIPALITIES

Undoubtedly, our many years of experience in spiritual deliverance have helped us understand many of the devil's tricks and strategies. The Bible talks about the different demonic categories. There are rulers, authorities, powers of this dark world, and spiritual forces of evil in the heavenly realms (Eph. 6:12).

As for the rulers or principalities, we could say that each city has a prince. The best example is found in the Book of Daniel. Although Daniel had prayed, he wasn't receiving an answer. After twenty-one days of seeking God's face, an angel told him, "Since the first day that you set your mind to gain understanding [Daniel prayed with his mind] and to humble yourself before your God [Daniel was praying and crying before God], your words were heard, and I have come in response to them. But the prince of the Persian kingdom resisted me twenty-one days" (Dan. 10:12–13). The struggle was so intense that the angel had to ask for help to overcome the adversary. It meant that the prince over Persia was detaining the answer or blessing that Daniel was so anxiously waiting for.

That same thing happens today. There are principalities, strongmen, who rule and try in every way they can to stop the work of God. They want to hold back the crusades and put obstacles in the way of those who need Christ. In order to accomplish this, they will come up with all sorts of snags.

It's important to understand that the battle needs to be won in the heavens, in the air; only then will we see the victory reflected on Earth. We therefore need to bind and cast out the demons, principalities, and powers. Once the victory is achieved in the heavens, the battle on Earth will be easier because there will be no opposition from the evil one. That is the reason why the apostle Paul says that our struggle is not against flesh and blood. Our struggle is against the rulers, the authorities, and the powers of this dark world—against the spiritual forces of evil in the heavenly realms. It is against these that the church fights.

We need to understand clearly that there are several hierarchies of spirits, and we need to know who it is we are coming against when we declare war on the devil. Let's bind the strongman, the prince of darkness, as Paul said in 2 Corinthians 4:3–4: "And even if our gospel is veiled, it is veiled to those who are perishing. The god of this age has blinded the minds of unbelievers, so that they cannot see the light of the gospel of the glory of Christ, who is the image of God." If the world doesn't believe, it's because it is influenced, bound, by the spirit of unbelief. Let's rebuke this spirit so that they can believe, so that this demon will let go of their minds and the light of the gospel of the glory of Christ can shine in their lives.

CAN EVIL SPIRITS CAUSE SICKNESS?

We read in the Bible about Jesus and the crippled woman. Jesus realized that she had a spirit of sickness and said, "Then should not this woman, a daughter of Abraham, whom Satan has kept bound for eighteen long years, be set free…?" (Luke 13:16). According to this passage, we see clearly that an evil spirit can cause sickness. But are all illnesses caused by demons? For many years people believed so. But in reality, this is not so. Let us explain and prove it.

In Luke 9:1, Jesus makes one of many statements about this topic. When He commissioned His disciples, He gave them power and authority to drive out demons and also to cure diseases. Look carefully; the Lord made a distinction between demons and diseases. That means that not all diseases are demons.

Every time I pray for the sick, I rebuke the spirit of sickness, but I also rebuke the disease. I was once invited to preach in a church in the city of Buenos Aires. When I finished preaching, I called out to the sick to pray for them. Many came. The Holy Spirit said, "Call people with cancer."

I did, and some ten or twelve people came forward. When I prayed for them, I rebuked the disease, saying, "Spirit of cancer, come out of these lives in the name of Jesus." At my rebuke, four of them fell, started to roll, and were foaming at the mouth. They were healed. Even those who didn't fall or move were also healed. God is sovereign! Those of us who think we know anything realize we know nothing and that we are just humble servants of a great God. Alleluia!

There are many causes of sickness. In the following chapters we will explain in more detail the importance and the power of forgiveness. Seventy percent of the people who suffer spiritual problems and end up in our tent of deliverance have hatred, anger, and roots of bitterness in their hearts. These are among the main causes of sickness and oppression in people's lives. The vast majority receive physical healing when they find inner healing through forgiveness.

Examine your heart. There may be hatred toward a spouse, a cousin, one of your relatives, a neighbor, a brother, or a sister. Hatred and resentment bring punishment. Many times they are the main reason for diseases that seem to have no origin. No matter the reason why you hate, Jesus forgave and told us to do the same. If we don't do it, we remain in condemnation and disobedience to His Word. Forgiveness is not a *feeling*; it is a *decision*. If you want to forgive, the Lord will help you to do it.

I have prayed for people ruined by diseases who have received healing the moment they finished praying and confessing forgiveness. It's awesome how God's power operates through forgiveness. Don't allow the devil to use your feelings to bring sickness into your life.

AUTHORITY TO DRIVE OUT DEMONS

The Lord Jesus affirmed that the church has authority to cast out and rebuke demons when He said, "In my name you will drive out demons."

You don't kick them out or cast them out by giving oil to the demonized person to drink.

The real mission the devil has in this world is to kill, steal, and
destroy. We need to believe and understand this. He will not stop
bothering us until the Lord takes us to be in His presence. That is his
work and his goal. But God has given us authority and has equipped
us through His Holy Spirit to undo the works of the devil in the name
of Jesus.

Many times we believe that it is God Himself who will do it (and
this is true; He has already done it all), but the Lord has given us the
authority and the mandate to continue the work He started. Therefore
we can't pray for a demonized person by saying, "Lord, set this person
free." His answer will be that He has already done that on the cross!
We have to take hold of the authority He has given us and drive out
demons in His name. God gave authority to all who believe, not to one
person in particular. We need to treasure His authority in our hearts.
Faith gives us authority.

I firmly believe in what Jesus told His disciples when they couldn't
drive a demon out of a boy. They asked Him, "Why couldn't we drive
it out?" (Matt. 17:19).

The Lord answered them, saying, "Because you have so little faith"
(v. 20). And He also said something else: "This kind can come forth by
nothing, but by prayer and fasting" (Mark 9:29, KJV).

So, what happened? Was the Lord contradicting Himself? No, of
course not; He never does. When someone has faith, he can move
mountains. But when the faith is weak, we need to seek the face of
God, because faith is a gift that comes from Him. It isn't a human
attribute; it's a gift from heaven. If you want faith, look for it, because
God "rewards those who earnestly seek him" (Heb. 11:6). If you have a
powerful faith, one that moves mountains, there will be no devil that
will be capable of resisting you. But if not, ask by prayer and fasting to
be filled by God's anointing, power, and authority.

We have to earnestly seek God today. The church needs to look for
the power, the anointing, and the grace of God. We need to search for
Him by spending time alone in His presence, on our knees, pouring
out our hearts and our souls to Him, with tears, asking Him to equip
us, anoint us, and increase our faith so we can do the work according
to His will. Evil multiplies, science increases, man turns away from

God, and I believe that the only way to bring people closer to God is through the anointing and the power of the Holy Spirit. We can only achieve this by searching for God.

But who has power? Everybody does. Maybe you're thinking, "But Carlos, you have more power than we do!" You're wrong; that's not true. I have been able to prove this a thousand times. We all have the same authority. Why? It's simple. For a long time I asked Jesus to give me power, and do you know what His answer was? He said, "I gave it to you already."

But it wasn't real to me until He took me to the Word where I read, "These signs will accompany those who believe..." I said, "OK, I read it."

But He said, "Read it again."

When I did, the letters seemed to shine.

God asked me, "Do you believe in Me?"

I said, "Yes, Lord."

Then He said, "Power is not manifesting in your life because you still don't believe Me."

It is one thing to believe in God; it is another thing to believe Him.

That's the secret: *to believe God.* Even if you just recently became a believer, if you have to take action, do it! Don't be afraid. Trust in God! If you stand firm on His Word, God's protection is over you. Don't fear! You will have power; God doesn't make any exceptions. Some will have more faith, others less, but God gave us authority to do His work on Earth. On the other hand, if you have been a believer for many years, and yet when face-to-face with the devil you are afraid, he will laugh at you.

You have to exercise faith every day. What does an athlete do? He exercises every day so his muscles will grow. What happens if he doesn't do it? His muscles will shrink. It's the same with faith. If you want your faith to grow and be strong, you have to put it to work every day, put it to practice. And when you see that what He says in the Bible becomes a reality in your life, your faith will grow and greatly increase.

One woman who accepted Christ experienced such a radical change in her life that an *umbanda pai* came to see me so I could pray for him.

"I have five *umbanda* temples," he said to me. "I'm *pai.* My ads are in magazines and newspapers."

During our conversation, I told him, "You are offering the needy something you don't have. You don't have peace; you don't have joy; you are ruined."

The man accepted Jesus Christ into his heart, together with his wife.

Thousands and thousands of people are deceived and seek God where He cannot be found! We are to blame. We know the truth and we keep it to ourselves. Let's take it to the streets and proclaim it and tell everybody, "Jesus Christ can change your lives! Jesus Christ heals! Jesus Christ restores marriages…gives peace…JESUS CHRIST IS LIFE!" If we don't do this, the devil will continue holding them in his power and carrying them to hell by the thousands every day.

If the church doesn't work, the crusades end up in failure. It's true that one cannot force people to attend the meetings, but you have to preach to them and go with them to the meeting place. Those who accept Christ will do it because you evangelized them first. All we do then is put a seal on them.

Paul tells us, "My message and my preaching were not with wise and persuasive words, but with a demonstration of the Spirit's power" (1 Cor. 2:4). He didn't go with words but with a demonstration of the Holy Spirit. That's why the faith of those who believed was not based on men's wisdom but on God's power. This is the fruit that will last.

When I talk about this passage and say that the gospel is not about *words* but about *power*, many say, "But the Bible says, 'Blessed are those who have not seen and yet have believed.'"

And God says to me, "Tell them you glorify Me with those who, by seeing, believed." I myself am one who believed in the gospel by the things I saw. If I had not seen, I would have not believed. And I know this is how it is for many.

During a forty-five-day crusade in the city of San Justo, in the province of Buenos Aires, there was a man who brought his wife every night, but he wouldn't come close to us.

On one of the last days of the crusade, the man was walking his little dog in the surrounding area while waiting for his wife to come out. He put the dog on the top of his car. When I started the final prayer and said, "Jesus, touch!" the dog fell down from the car, landing on its back. This man loved his dog very much and thought it was dead. In the meantime I was continuing to pray, saying, "Get up and walk."

Instantly, the little dog got up and started to wag its tail at its master. Crying, the man came running to the platform with the little dog in his arms, ready to accept the Lord. This sign was sufficient for him.

God wants souls to know Him. Then He will manifest Himself in different ways, using different methods for different people. Many times He will use us as His instruments to accomplish this.

The Bible says that we all receive the anointing of the Holy Spirit, but it's up to us to use it or not. We need to give God the freedom to unleash His power in us.

Chapter 6

THE DEMONIZED

CRUSADE AFTER CRUSADE, HUNDREDS OF PEOPLE MANIFEST demons. Every day, before preaching God's Word, I pray and rebuke all evil spirits that want to bring confusion and put obstacles in the minds of those who are going to hear God's Word. Read the story of Patricia, who was miraculously delivered in one of our crusades.

It all started on a Sunday in 1982. I was having lunch, and all of a sudden it felt as if someone were piercing my eyes. It hurt a lot. Then it felt as if I had sand in my eyes, and light hurt my eyes. I went to several eye specialists, but they couldn't find anything wrong with my eyes. But my sight was deteriorating gradually, and finally, I lost my eyesight completely.

I was so desperate that I went to see an *umbanda pai*, who told me that with his help I was going to recover my sight; what I didn't know then was that his god was Satan.

I believed him and followed his instructions very carefully. One morning I asked my mother for a white chicken, honey, and four white candles. With all this, I went to see the *pai*. I dressed up for a ceremony, putting on white garments. The people meeting with the *pai* wrapped a white cloth around my head. Then they gave me what they call a "blood bath"; they slit the chicken's throat and poured all that blood over my body. I didn't know or care what they were doing to me. I was only interested in getting my eyesight back.

I went back home, promising to come back the next day. And so I did. When I arrived, they spread honey on my head, and they washed me with previously prepared herbs. From then on, I started to see again, and the sunlight didn't bother me anymore. I started to put my trust in these people.

A few days later, I started to notice that I was losing my memory. Soon I had difficulty knowing where I was. When I went out, I would get lost, and I started to panic. I wasn't feeling well. I went back to the *pai*. He told me I needed another one of their treatments, one that would take care of my brains. According to him, somebody was trying to make me lose my mind. After their treatment, I felt well again. Some time later, he offered to let me work with him, but my mother was against this idea since I was only fourteen years old.

Months went by, and I continued in bondage. Every day I would follow many different *umbanda* and witchcraft rituals. I learned everything about virgins, saints, the *orixá* and the *exú*, how to distinguish the different colors, how to prepare the trays with the offerings, what candles to use, what color to use, and how many. They explained to me everything about the "*caboclo* Indians" (black dolls). I had to give cigarettes to these dolls so they could smoke with me. There were many other things that I'd rather forget.

Some time later, the friendship I had with the *pai* was broken, and I left. After this, my physical—and spiritual—condition was terrible. So I began visiting a parapsychologist for help. After a few treatments, I felt better again.

In 1987, I went to see a doctor, who told me I had whooping cough. They gave me medicine for it, but I only got worse. I would vomit everything I ate. At times I would choke. I thought I was dying. On December 2 of that same year, I was hospitalized with bronchopneumonia. I was extremely weak and had to stay in the hospital for eighteen days.

Something inside was constantly talking to me. I felt like somebody was chasing me; I was hearing noises and could see something walking around my bed—I was scared. I couldn't trust anybody. Whenever I told someone what was happening to me, they laughed and mocked me, or they thought that I was crazy. I had no strength left.

One Sunday, my family took me to Brother Annacondia's crusade in Buenos Aires. When Brother Annacondia started to pray and rebuke demons, I fell to the ground. They immediately carried me to the tent of deliverance. I was kicking, biting, and hitting the stretcher-bearers. At the second night's meeting, they took me back to the tent to pray for me again. I vomited chunks of snakes and frogs and was finally set free.

Today I thank God for His infinite love and mercy. And I thank my pastor who leads me in God's way. I thank my family, who had to endure all those terrible things of the past. I got rid of all the charms, necklaces, and dolls. I am really a new creature, faithful to Jesus who rescued me from the hell I was in.

—PATRICIA

The devil cannot stand to hear the name of Jesus, so during prayer one can hear screams coming from the crowd. Immediately, dozens of stretcher-bearers run to the different people who are shaking and screaming out of control. The brothers who work as stretcher-bearers have authority to rebuke Satan and to tell him to stop so they can transport the people to the place where counselors will pray for their spiritual deliverance.

Many times, by looking into people's eyes, I realize who is in charge of their life, who is the king of their hearts. The eyes express a lot of what we believe. The look in the eyes of an oppressed person is hard; they reflect a resistance to prayer. When I look into their eyes, I sense the intruder in their lives, usurping, resisting, hurting, wounding, and destroying what doesn't belong to him. But God has given us authority to set these people free from the devil.

In my church, whenever somebody who was demonized started manifesting, we would all throw ourselves onto him. The pastor as well as the deacons would rebuke the devil, all shouting at the same time. Now think; what would happen to you at work if the president, the vice president, the general manager, and the production manager all said, "No, no, no, do it this way...no, better this other way!"

You would surely look at them and say, "Excuse me; make up your minds, and then just one of you tell me what I'm supposed to do. When you shout at me all together, I can't obey any of you."

The devil is subject to authority; if I rebuke the devil and you do too, we neutralize our authority as we take it away from each other. If I say, "Devil, in the name of Jesus, go!" and the person next to me tells him to do the same, he will not do it. God has shown me that this is one of the reasons why, after days of shouting, often we still had no results.

I shouted because I wanted to drive out the demon. The other person did the same. Without realizing it, we were taking away authority from each other, and so the devil would not go.

What do we have to do? First of all, we need to respect each other's authority. As one prays, the other backs him up. When the one praying gets tired, he delegates the authority to the other and continues backing up that person in prayer. Then the devil, who is subject to authority, has to obey. But if we all give orders and shout together, he will not obey.

Many times, demonized people left the meetings without having been completely delivered. The next day they manifested the same demonic behaviors as they did before. Time after time the same thing happens. Today, when I see someone coming into the tent of deliverance for a third time, I ask why that person isn't free yet. In that case, the counselor can shout and rebuke the devil all night long, and nothing will occur. You can't go into a house if they don't open the door for you to come in. There are people who don't recognize they are in bondage, and so God will not break their free will. They are the ones who have to choose and decide what they want to do.

When people want to be set free, it happens right away. They don't have to come into the tent of deliverance more than once. If this happens, it's because something is not right. I remember a brother who, during one of the crusades, asked me, "Do you remember me?"

"No, I don't," I answered.

He then said to me, "I am the one who spent so many nights in the tent of deliverance in the city of San Martín."

Today, I give glory to God because that doesn't happen anymore. He has taught us a lot. God's teachings are practical and effective. When we follow them, our work is fruitful, and people receive and enjoy the freedom that exists in Jesus Christ without too much unnecessary racket or noise. The important thing is for us to work with wisdom and with the love of God and to use the authority correctly. This authority lies in the name of Jesus. When you say, "Devil, you go now in the name of Jesus!" the person is set free for the glory of God.

During a crusade in La Boca, a suburb of Buenos Aires, I was coming down from the platform after preaching when one of the counselors who worked in the tent came and told me, "Brother, come, there is a demonized man in the tent who says he is Beelzebub. You cast him out."

So I said, "In the Bible it says, 'These signs will accompany those who believe: In my name they will drive out demons,' so you have authority against Satan and against all the demons."

"Do you think so?" she said with hesitation.

"Yes," I insisted. "Tell Beelzebub to go out of that life in the name of Jesus."

When they finished praying for all the sick, this same sister came out of the tent to tell me, "Brother, it worked. The man is free."

Glory to God, the power is in *the name of Jesus.* He was with her, and He is with you. Jesus is with us. If we believe in Him and believe His words, we will have authority.

We have to depend on God. Many times there are things you don't know, and the Holy Spirit reveals them to you. The Spirit gives that gift of discernment to us when we ask, "Lord, what's going on?" He reveals it to us not only because He wants us to be victorious, but also because He wants us to learn to depend on Him.

Can the devil bind a church member? Many say that this is not biblical, that it can't be. In Luke 13:10–17, Jesus called the crippled woman a "daughter of Abraham." He recognized her as a daughter of God, someone who believed in God, and yet she had a demon. How could this be? We also believe that a Christian full of the Holy Spirit, living according to God's will and not living in sin, can't be demonized or have spiritual problems.

> We know that anyone born of God does not continue to sin; the one who was born of God keeps him safe, and the evil one cannot harm him.
>
> —1 JOHN 5:18

He who practices sin, be he a member or not of a Christian church, opens the door to the devil. Our leaders estimate that 30 to 40 percent of the people who receive ministry in our crusades are members of the church who have spiritual problems. When we pray for them, we don't ask the Lord why they are experiencing problems; we just simply minister to them.

The Lord called us to set people free so that they can reestablish perfect communion with Him. Then how can the devil enter into a life such as he did in the life of the crippled woman in Luke 13? We need to have that information in order to close the doors to Satan and cast him out forever, never to come back to torment a life. In the majority of cases where a person had a spiritual problem caused by Satan, there are roots from the past—pacts that are still unbroken, fears, jealousies, hatred, grudges, bitterness, sexual perversions, and other sins. These feelings are rooted in a bondage that won't allow them to enjoy an abundant life. Joy has to come into their lives and hearts. The Lord says He will bless His people with His peace.

There are two ways to live our Christian lives: in victory or in defeat. In the majority of situations it depends on the person. If people hide their weaknesses and problems and refuse to confess their sins to spiritual leaders who can provide help and break the devil's chains, they will never enjoy a lasting victory. Psalm 32:3 says, "When I kept silent, my bones wasted away."

One night during one of our crusades, every time I rebuked the devil from the platform, a woman in the audience began to manifest, shaking violently. But although we went to the tent of deliverance several times for prayer, she left unchanged each time. The counselors told me that she had accepted the Lord some time ago and was attending a church.

The next evening, the same thing happened again; when I rebuked the devil, she started to shake and scream. The Holy Spirit put the word *abortion* in my heart. He was letting me know something about this woman's life. I finally approached her and said, "Have you had an abortion that you have never confessed or repented of?"

That night, with tears of repentance, she confessed that she had had five abortions. She cried out to God to forgive her, and she was set free. Not only did God set her free, but that night she also received the gift of tongues.

Man Is Tripartite

Man is comprised of spirit, soul, and body. Let's examine some details of each one of these.

Spirit

In John 3:6 we read, "Flesh gives birth to flesh, but the Spirit gives birth to spirit." God's Spirit generates a new spirit in the believer. (See Ezekiel 36:26–27.) The Scriptures also tell us that God's Spirit is like the wind:

> The wind blows wherever it pleases. You hear its sound, but you cannot tell where it comes from or where it is going. So it is with everyone born of the Spirit.
>
> —JOHN 3:8

God's Spirit is like the wind—it has free movement and animated power—and so does everyone who is born of His Spirit. God has given a new spirit to each of us, and it is the core of an individual's life. The spirit is what distinguishes man from all other living creatures. This sphere of man's life is the one that receives the things from God:

> But it is the spirit in a man, the breath of the Almighty, that gives him understanding.
>
> —JOB 32:8

Soul

This sphere is comprised of the mind (psyche), the emotions (feelings), and the will.

> The soul who sins is the one who will die.
>
> —EZEKIEL 18:4

Body

The body is comprised of the five senses: hearing, sight, taste, touch, and smell. But now, who sins? The soul or the body? The body is the visible, but it is the soul that makes decisions through the will. The flesh reflects the desires of the soul. We can better understand this when we read 2 Samuel 11:2:

> One evening David got up from his bed and walked around on the roof of the palace. From the roof he saw a woman bathing. The woman was very beautiful…

Many times I've heard people say, "Oh, well, the flesh sins," trying to minimize sin. David saw Bathsheba, but he didn't commit sin just because he looked at her. Or is it that we sin every time we see a beautiful woman or hear a sweet woman's voice? I believe that the body's senses are like a sensor that transmits information to the soul. If David had looked at Bathsheba and continued to walk around without stopping, nothing would have happened. But David stopped, desired, lusted after her, and sent someone to get her: "Then David sent messengers to get her. She came to him, and he slept with her" (v. 4).

Here is where David's feelings, his emotions, his will, and his soul came into action, and he sinned. I believe that the senses cannot decide; the soul decides and consummates sin. The flesh carries out the desires of the soul.

> So I say, live by the Spirit, and you will not gratify the desires of the sinful nature. For the sinful nature desires what is contrary to the Spirit, and the Spirit what is contrary to the sinful nature. They are in conflict with each other, so that you do not do what you want.
>
> —GALATIANS 5:16–17

This strong opposition is because the Spirit wants to please God, and the soul and the flesh are opposed to pleasing God: "The sinful mind is hostile to God. It does not submit to God's law, nor can it do so" (Rom. 8:7).

YIELDED TO THE HOLY SPIRIT

There are two big risks in every Christian's life. The first is to believe that everything happens because of demonic activity. When we do this, we take our eyes from Jesus. The second risk is to believe that even if we are in sin or choosing to live our lives contrary to the will of God, we are totally immune to Satan—the worse thing he could do to us is oppress us. Consequently we neglect our spiritual lives, and we give him the possibility of ruling us. We believe that if we ignore him, this will keep him away. Don't be deceived; this is one of his most common tricks.

But how can a Christian have spiritual problems? Some say that where the Holy Spirit is, the devil cannot be. That's true, but don't forget that man is comprised of body, soul, and spirit. The Holy Spirit dwells in man's spirit—the Scriptures say that the Spirit of God dwells within and becomes one with man. When the Spirit comes, He begins to govern all the different areas of our life: the emotions, feelings, and the will. God will take everything we give to Him, but there are aspects of our lives that we take years to hand over to Him.

When is a person full of the Holy Spirit? When the Holy Spirit is in charge of all areas of a person's life. Then we can say that the person is filled with the Holy Spirit, and the fruits will prove it. If someone has yielded his or her emotions, feelings, and will to Christ, that person will exude Christ's love at every step. But this is not always the case, since many times people will not give control of certain areas of their lives to the Holy Spirit. The Spirit will not struggle to come into a person's spirit to rule.

If an area is not in Jesus's hands, in whose hands is it? What a question! I believe Satan can govern areas of our soul if we allow him to. That is where the struggle begins, because the Holy Spirit will not overpower a person's free will. When He has our whole being in His hands, He can govern the emotions, the feelings, and the will. Therefore, if there are aspects of our lives that are not yielded to Him, we have to hand them over. For example, let's consider our tempers. We have to tell God, "Lord, look at my temper; I don't want to get angry! Holy Spirit, take my rage. I renounce it, and I renounce anger in the name of Jesus!" We tell the Holy Spirit to rule that part of our lives so we can be filled with the power and love of God.

Finally, we need to stand firm. It's the simple end of every speech: "Now all has been heard; here is the conclusion of the matter: Fear God and keep his commandments, for this is the whole [duty] of man" (Eccles. 12:13). Once we do this, the devil will have to flee, and our house will be filled with God.

The devil walks around, saying, "Where should I come in today?" He goes by a house where people are listening to rock music and watching steamy television programs, and he says, "I'm coming in here." And he creates havoc there. Now what happens if he goes by your house and hears Christian music to which you are singing? Glory to God! Alleluia! He can't enter! In another house he hears people praying and seeking God. Then the devil says, "This place is not for me," and continues walking. Let's fill our lives and our homes with Jesus Christ. "Do not give the devil a foothold" (Eph. 4:27).

Remember this: if a person has problems, it is because he or she has opened the door to the devil. We need to know what the problem is so we can promptly take action, break the bondage, tell the spirit to come out, and close the door so the devil can never return to bring destruction. For this, we need to constantly use the knowledge God gives us through the Scriptures and exercise authority.

Chapter 7

SPIRITUAL DELIVERANCE

IN EVERY CRUSADE SERVICE, THERE ARE HUNDREDS OF MEN, women, and children who, after a few moments of prayer, start manifesting demons. Perhaps their bondage is due to magic, spiritualism, macumba, or false doctrines. These people's spiritual deliverance is necessary for them to be set free from their slavery to Satan's rule. The best way to minister to someone in bondage is by giving that person love—"not caressing the demons," but caring for the person's soul. People who have had their palms read or who have gone to a psychic to find out about what is to come need ministry, regardless of whether they are manifesting visibly or not. They may not be demonized—but oppressed, tormented, or possessed. If they have made pacts with the devil, these pacts will be still in force until they are severed or broken through deliverance.

One of the issues we have had to confront and train our counselors to handle has been ministry to homosexuals who have spiritual problems and need guidance and spiritual deliverance. Once, during one of our meetings in Argentina, a young man from the crowd started to shout at me, blaspheming the name of God with his words. Some time later, he came back to a crusade—this time to give testimony of what God had done in his life. This is his story:

When I was fifteen years old I became a homosexual. I took a partner, and he came to live with me at my parents' house. From that moment on, my home became hell. It was impossible to live there. My mother felt so much shame that she wouldn't go out of the house, and she died of depression soon after. My father started to drink and became an alcoholic. They both rejected me.

Later, I broke away from that relationship and tried to leave the homosexual life behind, but I couldn't. The idea of being a woman was already formed in me, and so I decided to continue in that path. I started to mix with homosexuals. I was getting worse and worse; now I not only was a homosexual but also a transvestite. I would dress up like a woman and work as a prostitute to make money.

But I got sick, and the doctors couldn't help me. A blood disease started to destroy me. It eventually developed into chronic rheumatism that affected my back, twisting it completely out of shape, and caused my leg to be dislocated. I was also going blind. The doctors couldn't find the right treatment for my disease, and the weekly vaccine shots they were giving me were to no avail—I was getting worse every day.

After nine years of intense suffering, I started to visit witch doctors and witches to find healing for my body, but everything remained the same. I even sent my picture to the most notorious sorcerers in the country, but nothing happened.

After much suffering, one night I decided to put an end to my life. I left my home and started to walk toward the train station. I was determined to throw myself under the train, but on my way there, a friend saw me. Realizing I wasn't doing well, my friend said, "Why don't you come with me? There's a crazy guy a few blocks from here that's talking about Jesus."

I was angry, and I told him to leave Jesus alone since He was dead, adding that I wasn't going anywhere. He insisted and insisted until he almost had to drag me there.

Once in front of the platform, the evangelist, Carlos Annacondia, started to preach. I shouted at him, "Leave God alone. If hell is for real, show it to me." But he continued preaching. At the end of the meeting when he came down from the platform to pray for people, a very nice lady took me to him, and I said, "I don't believe in God. If you can do anything for me, do it."

He looked at me and laughed. Then he said, "Don't challenge me. Challenge God." Then he gave me a hug and left.

When I went back home with my friend, something was happening inside of me...something was changing. When I opened the door, the first thing I did was to look for the Bible someone had once given to me. I went to the patio, knelt down, and cried, "Jesus, if You really exist, help me. I just can't go on like this. If You are real, I'm now giving my life to You." Suddenly, fire from heaven engulfed me. I opened my eyes and could see, my back straightened, and my legs were healed. But that's not all; the miracles continued. God set me free from homosexuality and transvestism. Now I go regularly to church and preach the gospel of Jesus Christ.

—JUAN

Homosexuality is not a disease; it is caused by an evil spirit that takes hold of a life. Leviticus 18:22 says, "Do not lie with a man as one lies with a woman; that is detestable." Homosexuality and other sexual practices are part of a list of abominations such as sexual relationships between close relatives, adultery, offering of children as a sacrifice to idols, and sexual relationships with animals. God sternly confronts such practices because they destroy the life of society, of the family, and of the people themselves. He clearly condemns all homosexual practice by either a man or a woman:

Because of this, God gave them over to shameful lusts. Even their women exchanged natural relations for unnatural ones. In the same way the men also abandoned natural relations with women and were inflamed with lust for one another. Men committed indecent acts with other men, and received in themselves the due penalty for their perversion.

—ROMANS 1:26–27

If homosexuality were a disease, God would not condemn it. Through these passages we see that it is sin. A high percentage of the people who have been delivered by God from homosexuality have shared with us that they had been either raped or abused sexually as children. Many times words such as "You are a sissy," said by parents with the intention to hurt a child, can enslave a boy to those statements. When Jesus comes into their lives, however, the evil spirit has to leave, and they are free. There is no need for any further treatment, I can assure you.

If you know anybody in this situation, talk to him about Christ! He can set him free. Jesus came to this world to save what was lost. You are among them; they and I are too. He loves them as much as He loves you and me. It is very important for them to know that somebody really loves them, someone who can transform their lives. And that someone is Jesus. They need Him—people are constantly discriminating against them, and they have no real love in their lives.

There is another powerful story of a young man who came up to the platform in a crusade. In front of five thousand people, he courageously shared the following story:

> My name is Luis, and I had been a homosexual and a transvestite since I was twelve years old. I used to dress up like a woman and was attracted to men. I practiced prostitution, and I never revealed my real identity to anybody. Once I came to your meetings, but nothing changed until that night when God healed me from a bad and incurable case of syphilis. That healing led me to believe in God, but I fell into even worse sin until I came back to this crusade.
>
> The first night after the prayer, I fell down, and when I came back to my senses I was in the tent of deliverance. When the counselor asked my name, I said, "My name is Luis." That really took me by surprise since I had never revealed my real name to anybody before. I had always used pseudonyms. That night, together with the counselor, I renounced all spirits of homosexuality and confessed all my sins to God. From then on I showed evidences of the change that took place in my life.
>
> The next day, I went to a men's hair salon for the first time. I had my hair and my nails trimmed. Every single night after that I came to the crusade, and every time I fell to the ground. Time after time they took me to the tent, until I finally felt completely free.
>
> For the first time I found my true identity, and I felt like a man. I changed the tone of my voice, my mannerisms, and even the way I sat. They advised me to burn my feminine clothing, and that's what I did. From that day on everything changed. I don't feel uncomfortable in front of the opposite sex, and I can really look at women. I feel free; I had an encounter with God, and He came to dwell in my heart.

God has the power to liberate those who manifest inclinations such as homosexuality, transvestism, and lesbianism. Clearly God did not create a third sex: "He created them male and female and blessed them" (Gen. 5:2).

Every person who wants to get out of abnormal sexuality of any kind, in coming to Jesus, finds the freedom he desires and through Jesus recovers the identity that God created in him.

Seven Steps Toward Spiritual Deliverance

As a church, we need to prepare ourselves to rebuke evil spirits and give advice to the person who has been delivered. So, what happens if we are right in front of a demonized person? How should we proceed, and what should be our attitude? There are seven steps we need to follow when we confront a demonic manifestation. Each one is very important.

1. Verify the demonic possession.

You do this by observing the reactions of those who are possessed. The way to externalize a demonic possession is through the following manifestations (there may be others):

- A mental block
- Violent reactions such as blows, kicks, and other things
- Blasphemies
- Incoherent talk
- Feeling of breathlessness
- Looks full of hatred or glassy, unfocused eyes
- Manifested oppression in some part of the body
- Vomiting
- Uncontrollable screaming

All these manifestations take place while we rebuke the demon in the name of Jesus. If you perceive any of these expressions or movements, take authority and bind the demon, saying, "Be bound in the name of Jesus." Both the human spirit and the demon are subject to our authority if we do it in the name of Jesus. If a person is lying on the ground and doesn't open his or her eyes, you have to address the human spirit and say, "Open your eyes in the name of Jesus." And the person will have to open his or her eyes. When a possessed person doesn't want to come back or talk to you, command them by saying, "Human spirit, come back and take control over your body in the name of Jesus."

One time our crusade was being held right next to a police station. Actually, our tent of deliverance was positioned only twenty meters from it. All of a sudden, one demonized man (a wild one) ran away from our tent, straight toward the police station. All the policemen who were standing at the door were watching the events. The demonized man was foaming at the mouth as he ran rapidly toward them. They were all so scared that, within a few seconds, the five of them went into their building and closed the door behind them. We said, "Satan, we bind you in the name of Jesus; stop!" Instantly the man fell flat on his face. Afterward, the astonished policemen came out of the police station and were looking around. Maybe they were thinking how good it would be for them to have the same kind of authority we had in order to stop any inmate from running away.

2. Exercise authority over the evil spirit.

This is the second step. All who have authority can expel demonic spirits. But we must not be afraid or have doubts. If so, we will fail. Let's not forget that we exercise authority by faith, and that the opposite of faith is fear and doubt.

When we give an order, the devil needs to obey. Of course, if you bind the devil in your own name and not in the name of Jesus, he will not obey. The only name he responds to is the name of our Lord Jesus Christ.

3. Bring the person back to awareness.

Once the demon is bound in the name of Jesus, exercise His authority by taking this third step. This is how it's done: "Human spirit, in the name of Jesus, take control over your mind and your body." The individual has to respond with his or her senses, and will, to this call.

4. Ask the individual if he wants to be set free.

The fourth step is asking the person if he wants freedom. Carefully explain to him what his problems are. That person is in deliverance, and he doesn't have a clue how he got there. By explaining his condition, we help him to make the decision to be set free. But if he doesn't want to be delivered, there's not much we can do for him.

Many times people have a pact with the devil that needs to be broken. If they don't, the devil will not want to come out, even with words such as these: "Devil, come out of this life right now." We need to know how the person arrived at this point. Ask questions and investigate to find out how he or she was possessed and any other details that may help in the process of deliverance. If the person says things like, "I went to a séance," "I made a blood covenant with a witch doctor," "I consulted with a witch," you have to say, "You made a pact, and you need to break it."

The person needs to say these words: "I renounce spiritism in the name of Jesus." It's that simple. Or if he is in that condition because he practiced mental control, guide him to say, "Father, I renounce mental control." He needs to renounce the specific sins he committed, and the one ministering with God's authority has to say, "I break this pact in the name of Jesus." And in this simple way, pacts are broken.

There was a woman who came for three consecutive years to our crusades. She was crazy and had been like that ever since the time someone she didn't know came into her house and cast a spell over her. She was so deranged that she couldn't live with her family any longer. She used to put white paper all over the house to prevent contamination, didn't allow her husband or children to get near her, and ate on a lid with her hands instead of utensils. She lived like an animal, didn't talk to anybody, and whined all day.

One day her sister brought her to the crusade and told me what was wrong with this woman. She was very short, her eyes were unfocused, and she was constantly gesticulating. Her sister was with her, holding her hand. I was very affected to see the condition she was in. I prayed for her with all that was in me. Several times I rebuked the spirit of witchcraft, and said, "Spirit of witchcraft, go!" But nothing happened. I was feeling very sorry for her; they had to travel two hours to come to the crusade and had to go back home very late every night.

One day as I was praying I saw her standing in line for prayer. When I saw her, I said to the Lord, "Please give me discernment; I really don't know what's wrong with her. Lord, may Your Holy Spirit guide me. I know that someone has cast a spell on her. But why doesn't she get free?" While praying for other people, I was also praying for her. Suddenly, tears started to roll down my cheeks, and as I was approaching her, I felt an incredible compassion from the Lord in my heart. I know that when God puts compassion in the heart of His children it's because something is about to happen. The Holy Spirit said to me, "Do you know what's wrong with her?"

"Yes," I replied. "It's a work of witchcraft, a spell."

"So what are you going to do?" asked the Holy Spirit.

"I don't know. I've already rebuked the spirit several times, and nothing happened."

Then God asked me, "Who are you?"

"A priest of God," I said.

"Who bound her?" He asked.

"A priest from Satan."

"And who has more authority?" said God.

"I do," was my immediate response.

"Then use it!" He ordered me.

I just stood there, so surprised. God was teaching me something I didn't know. I had rebuked the spirit of witchcraft, but I hadn't exercised authority to set her free. Then I approached the woman, put my hand upon her head, and said, "Satan, you who are in there, you know the authority I have because I am a priest of the Most High God. I undo all your works in this woman's life, and I order you to go. I set this soul free from the spirit of witchcraft in the name of Jesus." At that instant, the woman fell to the ground and was taken to the tent of deliverance, but she was already free. It was beautiful to see her hugging her sister and laughing as they left. Every time I see them joyfully worshiping God in the crusades, I give thanks to Jesus for His incredible love.

There are several different ways in which the devil can bind people. We have people come to us for deliverance who have submitted themselves to serve as priests in the occult, doing everything from horoscopes to black magic. Sometimes we don't realize the danger there is in some children's games such as Ouija boards or the cup.

We have seen young men bound after invoking satanic powers in the cup game. All such occultic games have an impact in the spiritual realm.

We have to be careful with the cartoons our children watch, such as *The Smurfs* or others that have characters using supernatural powers. These prayers try to take the children's minds away from the only true power, the power of God. The power behind such cartoons binds our children, and then come the consequences: rebelliousness, epilepsy, and other behaviors or manifestations that result from watching television programs that appear innocent but are not. Beware of cartoons that portray heroes from Greek mythology. The children unknowingly penetrate with their minds into those spiritual powers and then experience all kinds of problems that cause us to wonder what is going on with them.

We need to be very alert. The Bible says that Satan "prowls around like a roaring lion looking for someone to devour" (1 Pet. 5:8). All these little things I just mentioned don't seem very important, but in the tent of deliverance we have ministered to children bound by spirits who would manifest and talk to us, mentioning different cartoon or television series characters. That motivated us to alert parents about the dangers of these TV programs.

In the city of La Plata, in Argentina, some children were said to have seen little green dwarfs descending from a flying saucer. News about this spread all over the world, and people from several countries came to interview the children. Some time later, we ministered to some of them in our tent. The parents themselves brought them to us because of the problems they were having. Those children were tormented, and they started manifesting the moment they heard the name of Jesus.

We know how the devil operates. He dresses up like an angel of light, like an extraterrestrial being, in many ways, just to be able to destroy. He has a whole bag of tricks with which to deceive us and take our lives and those of our children. Let's pay attention and be alert.

One night when I finished preaching, I left the platform and went by the tent. It was really late. When I came in, I saw a young man on the floor with his arms extended. He appeared to be dead; the brothers praying for him were seated around him, exhausted. I realized the young man had not been delivered. When I looked at him, the Holy Spirit said, "Martial arts." I helped the young man to get up, and after sitting him in front of me, I asked, "Do you practice martial arts?"

"No!" he responded.

"Well, the Holy Spirit is telling me that there is a pact that you made with the martial arts while watching television. Did you make such a pact?"

"No!" he said again.

I know that the Holy Spirit doesn't lie; there was something he wasn't telling me. I asked him if he was violent, if he had a desire to destroy or to kill. He said yes to that. I prayed and said, "Lord, You are never wrong." In that moment, the name of a famous martial-arts champion came to my mind. There are many movies and television series that have been made with him. So I asked him again, "Do you admire such and such a person?"

The young man looked at me surprised, and said, "Yes! How did you know?"

"Do you want to be like him? Were you standing and practicing the same movements he did in his movies? Did you imagine yourself hitting your enemies to overcome them?"

"Yes!" he said, very surprised at each one of my questions.

"You have allowed those same evil powers that rule the life of that man to rule over you. Now you must renounce the authority that man has over you, renounce the martial arts, and renounce the pact you made with them without being aware of it."

That night we prayed together, we rebuked the demons, and the young man was set free. His whole countenance changed, and he exclaimed, "I finally have peace."

Think carefully about what you allow your children to watch on TV. Mine watch only Christian cartoons. They have more fun playing with their toys, drawing, or playing sports. They don't spend time watching things that, instead of being beneficial, are detrimental to them. Provide good entertainment for your children. Spend time playing with them. I know it's easy at times to allow the television to entertain them, but my personal advice to you is this: devote time to your children!

5. Pronounce words of renunciation.

The fifth step is the one that brings about freedom and deliverance. When people pronounce words of renunciation, we take the authority we have in the name of Jesus to break all bondages and to drive the demons out. It doesn't matter if there are two, three, ten, twenty thousand, a legion, or two legions. When all the ties and all the commitments the person had with Satan are broken, the enemy's activity is terminated. There is no reason for the individual to continue being possessed.

Renouncing is a very important matter—and not only for our children. Once we find out what has taken place in the life of a person, be it pacts or resentments, be it physical or spiritual bondages, we need to lead the person to renounce aloud, in a very specific way, the various things that may be binding him or her. Maybe you wonder why it has to be aloud. Satan is not omniscient, but God is. The devil doesn't know what you are thinking, but God does. Therefore you have to renounce every bondage aloud so Satan can hear you. He can't read your mind; he doesn't know your thoughts. He will only know when you speak it aloud. That's why it's important to listen much and talk little, because when we talk, the devil gets to know what's in our minds. He can insert thoughts into our minds, but he cannot read what's in our hearts. Proverbs 18:21 tells us, "The tongue has the power of life and death." If we say, "My father died of cancer, and so did my grandfather; I probably will too," be sure that it will be so.

Satan says, "See, Jesus, this person wants to die of cancer." He heard what we said.

If we declare, "I will live all the years to which a man on Earth is entitled. I will be healthy, and I will not get sick," the devil will try to look for a point of entrance but will not find it.

The only one who can come in and affect your life because of His authority over you is Jesus Christ—not the devil. But if you confess and proclaim defeat, defeat will overtake you because you are revealing with your own mouth what you want to receive. That's why when breaking a pact, it needs to be done with words from our mouth and in an audible voice. The Bible says:

That if you confess with your mouth, "Jesus is Lord," and believe in
your heart that God raised him from the dead, you will be saved.
For it is with your heart that you believe and are justified, and it is
with your mouth that you confess and are saved.

—ROMANS 10:9–10

Why is this? When we say, "Jesus, I accept You," the devil covers his
ears, but he still hears what we said. But if you just say it in your mind,
Jesus tells Satan, "This person is mine," but Satan says, "I didn't hear
anything." When we confess before God and His angels and those who
are not, "I receive Jesus and ask forgiveness for my sins," all the spiritual forces listen to this confession, and the power of Christ comes
into action.

People who have made a pact need to renounce it aloud, never in
the mind alone. They need to say, "Satan, I renounce you in the name
of Jesus. I renounce spiritism in the name of Jesus."

Then Jesus will say, "Did you hear that, devil? They renounced you.
You no longer have any authority over their lives; I'm taking them away
from you."

Once I was asked to pray for a woman in the city of Los Angeles.
She was insane; she couldn't even talk clearly at times. When the ones
who were ministering to her were finished, they came and told me,
"She renounced this, she renounced that; everything has been done,
but there is no change in her." So I laid my hands on her head and
said, "Satan, everything has been already done; now you have no more
reasons to keep her in your hands. I order you to go and to leave her
alone. I declare her free because she has renounced you, and you don't
have a place in her anymore. Woman, I declare you free." I turned
around and left, telling the prayer ministers to let her go home. They
helped her to her home, and the next day she was completely free. The
devil could not hold her any longer because he had lost his authority
over her.

In another crusade, a woman suffering with hemiplegia, who was
the wife of a military man from the city of Berisso, Argentina, came
to one of my first crusades. That night I rebuked all spirits of depression, of hemiplegia, and every demon. The woman fell to the ground,
and at that moment she heard a voice saying, "I have to leave. I have
to leave; they drove me out." But in reality, he had not left. That night

while sleeping, she felt something detaching from her body, and the hemiplegia disappeared.

Sometimes the spirit will not leave right away, but eventually it will have to go. You have to say, "It's done." Confess the Word of God. When everything has been done correctly, the pacts have been broken, and nothing remains hidden, the person has to be free and delivered. If not so, it's because there are still things that remain covered and need to be brought out into the light.

Many times, because of shame, people do not want to confess situations or sins of their past, but finally they will say, "I remember I once made a pact...my husband was seeing another woman so I went to a warlock...he cast some spells...gave me this or that...and I did that." Such pacts need to be broken. When all the ties that bind you to the devil are broken, there is no reason why he should stay one more minute, ruining your life and your home.

6. Give thanks to God for the deliverance and ask to be filled with the Holy Spirit.

The sixth step is to tell the people to give thanks to God for His deliverance and to pray to be filled with His Holy Spirit. We do this in order to bring His presence to dwell in our homes and in our lives.

There are a few recommendations in relation to our ministry of deliverance. There should never be two or three men ministering to a woman who is alone, not in the church or in any other location; the ministry should be mixed. Let's see an example. What happens when a man goes to church with his wife for the first time and she manifests demons? They take her away to the place where they do counseling and deliverance. After a few minutes, the husband starts to worry and begins to look for her. The ushers take him to the place where she is receiving ministry. As he comes into the room, he sees three men around his wife. One is holding her by the arm, the others by the shoulders. When the husband sees this, he says, "What is this? What is going on here?" Because of the difficulties such an experience could cause, it is important that another woman be present helping in the situation. It's not because I distrust the leaders or the counselors that I make this recommendation—I know they minister with the right intentions in Christ—but it's because of what others may think.

7. Verify the effectiveness of the deliverance.

The seventh and last step is to determine if the deliverance was effective. After people are delivered, they become very relaxed; they cry with joy. There is a sense of happiness, a change of mood, a sweet and peaceful look, and deep sighs. They don't reject the name of Jesus anymore, but instead they pronounce it with freedom. They now confess freedom and declare that what happened was done in the name of Jesus. At the end of the deliverance, the team needs to pray and glorify the name of Jesus, ascribing to Him and Him alone all the glory and all the honor.

These steps are not a strict method for ministering deliverance. These pieces of advice are the result of our own experience in this field throughout many years of ministry. I believe undoubtedly that the pastor of each congregation is the one who needs to direct each section of ministry and counseling. He, better than anybody, will tell you exactly what steps to take to be able to work in communion with the rest of your family, which is your church.

Chapter 8

THE DANGERS OF
THE OCCULT

THE FOLLOWING STORY SHARES THE MIRACULOUS conversion experience of a young man who had been deeply entrenched in the occult. God set him free from the bondage of Satan.

I studied clinical psychology at the University of La Plata, in Argentina. I also took courses on graphology and graphic tests. I worked for nine years in four psychiatric hospitals, in the rehabilitation of psychotics and with some other disciplines.

I was taught that knowledge is power. I craved to be rich in knowledge so I could be noticed and stand out among my peers. When I finished my studies, I decided that the area of scientific knowledge was sort of limited and very competitive. If I became a teacher of the occult, of astrology, parapsychology, folk medicine, and Eastern religions, I could dazzle people with the secrets of darkness. I wanted to be mysterious, deep, and seductive—a mixture of psychotherapist, guru, and sage. The supernatural and the mystical fascinated me.

Eventually, people who were lost fell into my trap. I used to seduce them with spiritual, ancestral, and esoteric discussions. My vanity would gleam. I was convinced I knew everything. Many had faith in me, they needed me, they followed me, and they finally ended in a life similar to mine: empty, but with an appearance of order; senseless, but with the illusion of being well planned; dissolute, but with an independent and modern appearance. It was an awful life, under the disguise of a temperamental personality; a fearful life, covered by a defiant, menacing attitude, always ready to attack.

For a long time I did astral charts and taught astrology, applying it to psychotherapy. I was an instructor in Eastern meditation and an investigator of some occult and parapsychology issues. I searched for God in all the Eastern religions, and I didn't find Him. For nine years I worked in the rehabilitation of psychotics in four hospitals: Melchor Romero, Borda, Estévez, and Moyano, all in the city of Buenos Aires. But I was expelled from all of them because I was against their electrical, surgical, and chemical treatments. So I started to work as a psychotherapist in my own home. I introduced myself as a psychologist so that people would not call me a healer. Some said that I had paranormal powers; I liked that and believed it. In reality, I was just an imposter, the blind leading the blind.

After years of investigating the truth about teachers, gurus, healers, and psychics, I realized that even though there were some stimulating and psychosomatic effects, none of them produced real change—that is, miracles. The results of their powers were deceitful and apparent. I told my followers, "I can only teach you what I have discovered in my search." This honesty captivated them even more.

They asked me many times about who God was, and I would say, "I only know Him through stories." When they asked about the devil, I would say, "I have seen him manifest in people, in some of my clients. I can assure you he is real."

Surprisingly, there were a lot of young people coming to me for private instruction on "knowledge and power in the occult." They were ready to pay anything to gain that knowledge. I taught them to meditate and to transfer energy. I was working all week, even Saturdays and Sundays. I was at the top, my dreams had become a reality, and success and fame were at the door. So, at thirty-seven years of age, I had fame, money, and success.

One Friday night in mid-October 1984, together with a group of psychologists, some advanced students, and other professionals, we decided to investigate what was taking place in Carlos Annacondia's crusades. Initially I didn't want to go, but my friends forced me to. We wanted to see his techniques and the powers he used. In front of a crowd, Carlos Annacondia preached fervently in the power of the Holy Spirit. I had never seen anything like it.

In the beginning, I was looking for subtle hypnotic induction techniques, paradoxical messages, and the emotional leading of crowds. But the power of God was manifesting with simplicity and transparency.

During the meeting, the sick were invited to come up front so they could receive prayer. I had been suffering from hereditary, incurable hay fever for a long time, so I decided to go up front and see if the signs and wonders were for real. Suddenly, a cry erupted from the inside of my being. I asked God for His salvation and for the love that I had never known. Annacondia said that if I believed that God was the only true God, if I accepted Jesus as my Lord and only Savior, if I repented of all my sins and renounced all wisdom except the wisdom that comes from God, I would be saved, reconciled to God, and healed. Right then and there I fell to the ground a broken man—a man of the world's knowledge, conceited, one who had worked so hard to reach a place of notoriety in the world. I believed Annacondia's words, cried, and asked God for forgiveness from my sins. For the very first time I understood what compassion is all about—loving others in spite of their wretchedness.

Later I could understand how Satan had used me as his instrument even though I had never searched for him or made any deliberate pacts with him. When I learned the Scriptures, however, I realized that my life was corrupted, sick, and heading toward death.

Blessed be our Lord Jesus who showed me His love! He didn't look at my malice or the many lives I had pushed into the abyss. He rescued me as He does all who come to Him, surrendering like a child, without conditions or demands! I never suffered from hay fever again.

At the end of October of that same year, I went to another of Annacondia's crusades. That night he said, "Let no one be found among you…who practices divination or sorcery, interprets omens, engages in witchcraft, or casts spells, or who is a medium or spiritist or who consults the dead. Anyone who does these things is detestable to the LORD" (Deut. 18:10–12). At that moment I realized how deep in sin I had been and how opposed to the work of God.

The next day I woke up early, feeling very sick, nauseous, dizzy, sneezing, coughing, shivering, and with cramps and spasms. I thought I had food poisoning; I felt as if I were dying. Something was squashing me against the bed, and my body felt like lead. All kinds of crazy ideas were rushing through my mind—painful memories and sins, but especially lies. Out of my inside came groans, hoarse voices, and grunts. I thought I was going crazy. After forty-five endless· minutes, I remembered how Annacondia rebuked the demons. I grabbed on to God with all my strength, and out loud with authority I said, "Evil lying spirit of false prophets, in the name of Jesus Christ of Nazareth, I bind you and command you to come out of my body, come out of my soul, and let go of my spirit. In the name of Jesus, abandon my life and never come back. My heart belongs to God, my Father." Afterward, I asked the Holy Spirit to take control of my tongue and to not let me be deceived again. Just a few minutes later I started to feel better. I wasn't cold anymore, I felt light and rested, and I fell asleep. When I got up and went out, a friend saw me and said, "You look terrible!"

"I had a rough night," I simply said. I didn't want to explain what had happened to me.

"However," said my friend, "you look brighter; your face looks cleaner and younger."

That same evening my friend and I received the baptism of the Holy Spirit. Behind the platform, with our arms raised, we started to speak in tongues. God set me free from the forces of Satan! Today, I'm committed to announce the good news, save the lost, and strengthen the weak in the faith in the name of our Lord Jesus Christ and for the glory of God.

—BASILIO

DEMONIC FORCES

When we talk about the spiritual forces of evil, demonic deliverance, spiritual oppressions, and demons, we are talking about all the demonic forces that stalk this world. (See 1 John 5:19.) He who ignores the truth is exposing himself to many dangers. One of them is the occult. This is a lie of the enemy that takes different forms in order to deceive those who are looking for answers and who have physical and spiritual needs. It is significant that in this desperate search for answers to life's questions, people take the wrong path. One of the reasons is that the church doesn't provide the answers for which they are looking. Therefore people start exploring the supernatural—witchcraft, sorcery, spells, and idolatry.

The science of the occult has devastated not only Argentina but also Latin America and many other parts of the world. Some so-called "first world" countries have been also deceived by these lies. The Word of God says, "There is a way that seems right to a man, but in the end it leads to death" (Prov. 14:12). We try to solve life's problems through quick and easy miracles. We don't want anything to be difficult, and of course we don't want any commitments or a change of life or attitude. We want magic.

When it comes to searching for God, many people find excuses. The reality is that God demands a lot of man—holiness and obedience among other things. He also demands respect for His will. So it seems easier to surrender to Satan, to the occult, and to whatever demonic experience there is on Earth. But Satan will also have demands. He will ask for certain things from us that we will not be able to deny him.

I once saw an ad in some esoteric magazine offering a cross that, according to claims, would bring you good luck and help you win the lottery. If you bought this cross and didn't win the lottery, the magazine promised to return your money. I'm sure many believed this lie and bought the cross. The same magazine also offered a good luck pyramid. It was supposed to help people get rich and healthy. Other ads said, "Rub the Buddha's belly and you will get rich; all your problems will be solved." They offered another cross to hang at your door that would bring peace, happiness in your marriage, and money for the rest of your life. Another ad promised to secure your future through sacred white-magic rituals performed according to your zodiac sign.

These are some of the things the devil offers to those who look for solutions and answers in the wrong places. Many people with problems go to witches, sorcerers, magicians, astrologers, and psychics. They have somebody read the tarot cards to them, thinking that God will speak to them through the cards. Please know that God condemns all these occult practices.

Probably you have noticed that many wealthy people have their own psychic—in other words, their own private witch. Some of the presidents consult them before making an important decision. This is very common; they want to know if their decision is the right one and what's in the future.

God doesn't approve of any of these things. He totally rejects them since they are satanic practices. My advice to you is not to waste your money and not to be in enmity with God. He doesn't dwell in those places, and He detests whoever practices those things.

Maybe you wonder why I say these things. Because the Bible talks about them. Only the Scriptures teach us the will of God. If you want to know the future, go to the Word of God. It teaches us what God wants for us. If you are practicing the occult, stop, get away from those practices, and draw near to God and His Word. You also need to leave sin behind—that is, whatever displeases God.

God's Warnings Against the Occult

Many men and women don't want to accept Jesus because they know that the works they are performing are evil and that if they draw near to the light, which is Jesus Christ, those works will be exposed. So they prefer to remain in darkness.

Let's take a look at what God says about some of these occult practices in the Bible.

Astrology

In regards to the "astrologers and stargazers" and those who predict the future, God says:

> Surely they are like stubble; the fire will burn them up. They cannot even save themselves from the power of the flame. Here are no coals to warm anyone; here is no fire to sit by.
>
> —Isaiah 47:14

Christians should not consult the horoscope or have any interest in the zodiac signs. This is from the devil.

Spiritism

Let's see what the Bible says about this:

> A man or woman who is a medium or spiritist among you must be put to death. You are to stone them; their blood will be on their own heads.
>
> —Leviticus 20:27

These words are from the Bible; it's not me saying this—it's God Himself. Many people talk to the dead. This is a common practice for the spiritists and mediums. Other people pray to the dead.

Divination

God talks about some other practices in Deuteronomy 18:10–12:

> Let no one be found among you who sacrifices his son or daughter
> in the fire, who practices divination or sorcery, interprets omens,
> engages in witchcraft, or casts spells, or who is a medium or spir-
> itist or who consults the dead. Anyone who does these things is
> detestable to the LORD, and because of these detestable practices
> the LORD your God will drive out those nations before you.

In His infinite mercy, God also says that all who look for answers
in witches, sorcerers, and witch doctors do this because of ignorance.
That's why we need to read the Word of God, to know which path to
take. "There is a way that seems right to a man, but in the end it leads
to death" (Prov. 14:12).

LET'S WALK IN THE LIGHT

Many times we do bad things because of lack of knowledge. We may
think we are doing what is right, but we are not. The Word of God is
clear, and now that we know it, we need to walk according to its truth.
Many times in our daily lives we do things like try to heal the "evil eye"
or an upset stomach with methods that only witch doctors would use.
You say, "But I do it in the name of God!" Have you ever realized in
whose name you are doing them? Another example may be the powers
handed down from fathers to sons on the night of December 24. This
is not of God. If your child has an upset stomach, just put your hand
on his forehead and say, "Jesus, touch my child and heal him." He will
heal him without you having to cast any spells. All that is nothing but
works of darkness, witchcraft, and sorcery.

All these practices are very common in Latin America. If we have
inherited any practices of sorcery or witchcraft, we need to abandon
them in the name of Jesus. God detests all these things. He teaches
us in His Word which path we need to take. If you used to participate
in these practices, ask God right now to forgive you; never go back to
them again.

We try to solve our problems, but many times we don't know what
caused a certain disease or why we have so much pain in our lives.

Maybe you have a broken home and don't understand why, so you decide to go to see a witch, sorcerer, or spiritist to find a solution.

We need to understand this very important truth: The true cause of your conflict is *sin*. It's our rebellion against God. So first of all, let's recognize that we are sinners and that we need God's mercy and favor. Then we will be able to come into His presence and say, "Lord, I am clean now by the blood of Jesus Christ." Then, as His children, we can claim the promises we find in His Word.

You may be thinking, "But I've never renounced God!" In some ways, this may be true, but the Bible says that we turned our backs to God when we did what wasn't pleasing to Him. All rebellious acts, transgressions, and disobedience to God, His precepts, and His commandments are sin. That means that we all sin unknowingly every day by doing things that are not pleasing to God. But He wants to forgive us. Jesus said He didn't come to condemn us but to seek and save those who were lost. He wants to reconcile with you.

Once you turn back to God, never leave Him again. Don't ever trust in witchcraft, horoscopes, or spiritism again. The world promises many evil and sinful things, and we are deceived. Don't allow this to happen! Jesus wants to change your life! Don't perish because of lack of knowledge. Only in Jesus will we find answers and hope. His hand of love and mercy is extended to all those who need Him.

> Be faithful, even to the point of death, and I will give you the crown
> of life.... be holy; without holiness no one will see the Lord.
> —REVELATION 2:10; HEBREWS 12:14

I remember a time when I used to get dirty with oily substances at work. Therefore I would go back home in the dark so nobody would see me. If I was clean, I didn't mind walking under the lampposts. So it is with sinners; when their souls are dirty, their consciences are also. So they will stay in the darkness. If they come to the light, their works will be seen, and they will be scolded. This is one of the reasons why they don't want to come near Jesus. They know that if they do, they will have to leave their bad deeds behind. They choose to stay in sin and wickedness, doing whatever they like to do while hiding in the darkness.

I'm sure you've never gone to a wedding all stained and dirty. You probably always wear your best clothes for the occasion. So it is with us; we need to be clean and ready to be in the wedding feast of the Lamb. No one who is dirty will be allowed to participate; that's why we need to make ourselves clean and holy and seek God with all our hearts and with sincerity. If we love Jesus, we need to be ready and prepared, because we know He is coming soon to get His church, and we will be in the wedding with Him.

Chapter 9

THE POWER OF FORGIVENESS

URING ONE OF MY FIRST CRUSADES, SOMEONE approached me asking if I could go to their house to pray for their mother. When the meeting was over, I went to see this lady, who was very sick. When I arrived, I found a crippled woman in bed, suffering from chronic asthma that affected her lungs. She was doing very badly, literally withering away, dying bit by bit.

The first thing I did was talk to her about Jesus and His salvation. When I finished, I helped her pray the confession of faith, and she received Christ in her heart. I then prayed for her, but I didn't feel the blessing of God reaching her. It was strange. I prayed and asked God what was going on. He said that this woman's heart was full of hatred, and His blessing could not reach her unless she could forgive.

So I decided to ask her directly, "Whom do you have problems with? Whom do you need to forgive?"

She told me that she had no problems, that she had a good relationship with those around her. I knew she was lying; God had confirmed something to me, and He doesn't lie. So I said, "Ma'am, you are not telling me the truth." As I was saying that, I felt in my heart that she had issues with her daughter-in-law. So I asked her daughter, "How many daughters-in-law does your mother have?"

"Two," she said.

"And what are their names?" I asked.

"One is called María Rosa and the other one, Ester," she responded.

With that information, I went to talk to the lady again and said, "How is your relationship with your daughter-in-law María Rosa?"

"Ah," she said with a smile, "María is a sweetheart. She comes twice a week with the grandchildren, and she brings me cake. She is a real example of what a daughter-in-law should be."

"And what about Ester?" I said.

Silence. I repeated the same phrase four more times and nothing. She wouldn't speak to me.

Then suddenly she said, "Don't even mention her name. She is a snake. She took my son away and doesn't allow my grandchildren to come and visit me. I hate her! I will never forgive her for what she did to me!"

In that moment she confirmed what God had told me, and so I tried to help her understand what was wrong with her.

"Do you know what is going on here? You are dying because your heart is full of hatred and resentment."

"I don't care. I'm not going to forgive her, even if it kills me," she angrily replied.

"But God is speaking to you, saying that if you don't forgive, that hatred in your heart will end up killing you," I said.

"I'm sorry, Pastor, but I don't feel like doing it."

I understood. There are times when it isn't easy to forgive someone who has hurt us so deeply. I've heard many stories of people who were abused as children. Others were raped, betrayed, attacked. All these terrible things hurt people's hearts very deeply.

Maybe those who have hurt us don't deserve our forgiveness. But we need to realize that we have committed even worse sins against our Lord Jesus Christ, and yet He says, "Father, forgive them, for they do not know what they are doing" (Luke 23:34).

I explained to this lady that forgiveness is not a feeling but a choice. If we had to "feel" like forgiving, we would probably never do it. I tried to help her understand this truth, and then we prayed together. I took her hand and asked her to repeat after me, "Lord, I forgive Ester! Lord Jesus, I forgive Ester!"

She had to make a huge effort to say these words, but she finally did. She repeated several times, "I forgive Ester, in the name of Jesus."

As she did this, tears started welling up in her eyes. The Holy Spirit had penetrated into her hard heart and was softening it. Crying, she said to me, "I feel like something lifted from my heart and now I am free."

"Did you forgive Ester?" I asked.

"Yes," she said, "I did."

After this, the healing started to flow. After three long years of not being able to walk, she got up and took a few steps. Everybody in that room witnessed *the real power of forgiveness.*

As We Have Forgiven...

> Forgive us our debts, as we also have forgiven our debtors....For if you forgive men when they sin against you, your heavenly Father will also forgive you. But if you do not forgive men their sins, your Father will not forgive your sins.
> —MATTHEW 6:12, 14–15

These verses in the Gospel of Matthew teach us what God's spiritual laws are that allow men to have access to His goodness and mercy. Many times we can't obtain God's gifts, or maybe we ask and have no answer. This is because we fail to obey His spiritual principles written in His Word.

Let's examine this legacy in greater depth so God's multiple benefits can reach our lives. I believe the Lord's Prayer is the best-known prayer in the world, but unfortunately it is also the most neglected. Let us take a look at part of the passage in Matthew 6:9–13 that we're examining.

"Forgive us our debts"

The Bible says we have a debt, and it's with God. Now then, what is the price of this debt? Can we pay it in cash? Remember God said that the wages of sin is death. He put a price on man's soul, and if we could get the money to pay for it, we would. But the Scriptures tell us that the soul of man is worth more than gold or silver. This means that we can't buy God's forgiveness. Many people would like to think that they can; when they die, they leave their money and possessions to the church so the church members will pray for them once they're gone. Let me tell you, though, God is not a merchant; we cannot buy His forgiveness or pay Him for His sacrifice on the cross. So man has to pay with his own life for his rebellion and disobedience. That means that the price of sin is death.

But when God saw that the whole human race was lost and that they all had to die, He sent Jesus to Earth, without stain and without sin, so that all who believed in Christ's justice would not be lost and die but would receive life. He didn't send Him to condemn the world, but so the world could be saved through Him. Therefore, just as sin entered the world through one man (Adam), and death through sin, so through Jesus life and blessing came in. When Jesus died on the cross, He fulfilled the plan and perfect will of God for man. On the cross, Jesus said, "It is finished." They all see Him crucified, but only a few know that He paid the debt that man has with God.

Christ is our mediator. When we get to heaven, we will carry with us the spiritual receipt that He put into our hands when we received Him in our hearts. Do you know what it says on that receipt? "Father, I paid Carlos's debt with My life and with My blood." This receipt is not written with ink, but with the blood that Jesus of Nazareth poured out for us on the cross. This means that if you give your life to Jesus, you don't owe anything any longer, because the gift of God is eternal life in Christ Jesus our Lord.

"As we also have forgiven our debtors"

This is the second part of the passage we are examining. According to all we have already discussed, the Scriptures are clear, and they openly declare that to receive God's forgiveness, we also need to forgive. When God forgives us, we are reconciled to Him and receive His salvation. If we don't obey this law, we lose God's forgiveness and His blessing. We also risk the salvation that Jesus freely gave us through His death on the cross of Calvary.

Day after day we see people with faces full of bitterness and anger. Hatred not only hardens the heart, but it also hardens our features. When we are spiritually upset, it shows all over our faces, and eventually it will start to wear our bones away. It affects our physical well-being. The Bible says, "When I kept silent, my bones wasted away" (Ps. 32:3). Hatred and resentment wound our souls and our hearts. If we don't heal those wounds completely, they will continually bleed. For years we carry grudges and a desire to pay back those who have hurt us in the past. If we don't allow God to intervene and heal us, we will be forever scarred.

Every feeling of anger, hatred, or resentment is an open door to the devil. These feelings, once under the devil's control, bring about suicides, depression, madness, and every kind of disease. Seventy percent of the people who come into our tent of deliverance are demonically possessed, but most of their spiritual problems are due to a lack of forgiveness.

In the Book of Ephesians, the Lord teaches us the following: "'In your anger do not sin': Do not let the sun go down while you are still angry, and do not give the devil a foothold" (Eph. 4:26–27). It doesn't say we can't get angry, but God doesn't want that anger to last overnight. Every night before we go to sleep, let's straighten things out with the Lord and also with those we may have hurt or offended that day.

If throughout our lives we have made mistakes and sinned against God, He is faithful and just and will forgive us our sins. He says, "Their sins and lawless acts I will remember no more" (Heb. 10:17).

Many people, even Christians, don't realize how important it is to forgive. But for God, to hate a brother is the same as killing him. "Anyone who hates his brother is a murderer, and you know that no murderer has eternal life in him" (1 John 3:15). Do you now understand what I am talking about? God says that anyone who claims to be in the light but hates his brother is still in the darkness. (See 1 John 2:9–11.) But He also says that if we love our brother, we live in the light and there is nothing in us to make us stumble.

Read carefully, my dear brothers and sisters. I'm not saying these things; God is. In 1 John 4:20 we learn that if we love God, yet hate our brother, we are liars. For if we can't love our brother, whom we have seen, how can we love God, whom we have not seen? Therefore this is the command: "Whoever loves God must also love his brother" (v. 21).

So don't be silent any longer. Don't keep on hiding this feeling that has been tormenting you for so many years. Maybe this is the barrier in your heart that has been stopping that long-awaited blessing from reaching your life. So confess your sins and repent; you will find reconciliation. There is no better thing than this.

FORGIVENESS BRINGS RECONCILIATION

On several occasions I've talked to people who had a hard time forgiving themselves for their bad choices or mistakes committed in the past. I've found others who resented God because they believed He had punished them with sickness.

The apostle Paul says the following with regard to forgiveness:

> And what I have forgiven—if there was anything to forgive—I have forgiven in the sight of Christ for your sake, in order that Satan might not outwit us. For we are not unaware of his schemes.
> —2 CORINTHIANS 2:10–11

If those who have wounds and roots of bitterness in their hearts don't fulfill the spiritual law of forgiveness, they give the devil an advantage and open a door to his schemes. All these are obstacles and struggles that Satan puts in the lives of those who have not given everything yet to the Lord, including their hatred and anger.

We know that Satan has come to steal, kill, and destroy, and that in the last days he has launched millions of demons to bring enmity among men. He has succeeded in bringing division between parents and children, between husbands and wives, between mothers-in-law and daughters-in-law, between friends, and between neighbors. He knows that if we fight and don't forgive, we'll stop God's blessings from reaching our lives.

The apostle Paul teaches us in Romans 5:10–11, "For if, when we were God's enemies, we were reconciled to him through the death of his Son, how much more, having been reconciled, shall we be saved through his life! Not only is this so, but we also rejoice in God through our Lord Jesus Christ, through whom we have now received reconciliation." When we receive Christ in our hearts, we are reconciled to God. And God, who reconciled us to Himself through Christ, has given us the ministry of reconciliation—and not just reconciled to Him, but also to all those who have offended and hurt us in the past.

The word *reconciliation* comes from the Latin word *reconciliatio,* and it refers to "the act of restoring broken relationships." It also translates to the Greek word *katallage,* which means "to change completely." Jesus provides the best examples of forgiveness and reconciliation. We see Him forgiving Judas, Peter, and those who crucified Him. Of these

He says, "Father, forgive them, for they do not know what they are doing" (Luke 23:34).

The same Holy Spirit who anointed Jesus is the One who abides in us today. At times, when preaching about forgiveness, I hear people shout, "Lord, I forgive!" In that very moment they receive the miracle they have been asking for and are filled with the Holy Spirit. Let me give you an example: If we want to fill a bottle with water, but we immerse it in water with a top on, hours can go by and the bottle will remain empty. You have to remove the top, and the bottle will get filled. The same happens in our lives; you need to forgive. Remove the top that doesn't allow the Spirit of God to freely flow in your life.

In 1994 I was invited to the annual conference of the Danish Assemblies. I preached on the power of forgiveness. There was a young man on crutches who caught my attention. He came up to the altar and shouted while crying, "I forgive my father. Lord, I forgive him." A few minutes later, I saw him throwing the crutches on the floor and running up the platform to give his testimony. God had healed him!

If your brother has sinned against you, endure and forgive him. Understand that with the measure you use, it will be measured to you. Mark 11:25 says, "And when you stand praying, if you hold anything against anyone, forgive him." The secret lies in what we confess. We may not have the ability to go and see the person we need to forgive—maybe that person is already dead or lives far away—but we can confess our forgiveness before God, pronouncing that person's name. For example, we can say, "Lord, I forgive John!" God is listening to you, but so is the devil. The Holy Spirit will fill your heart with love and heal every wound. Then the devil will see your obedience to God and will have to stop tormenting you.

The Lord forgave Judas's betrayal, Peter's denial, those who put Him on the cross, and also all of your sins and mine. Think and meditate upon these words. Ask the Holy Spirit to minister to you, to visit those places in your heart that are in darkness, and to bring to the light all the wounds that you have been covering and hiding for so many years in your attempt to forget.

It's your choice; don't wait any longer. If you don't forgive, God can't bless you. Restore the broken relationships in your heart, and you will be filled with many blessings from our glorious Lord.

Part Four

"THEY WILL SPEAK IN NEW TONGUES..."

Chapter 10

BAPTISM IN THE HOLY SPIRIT

WHO HAS THE ABILITY TO CHANGE PEOPLE'S LIVES? Nobody can truly bring a radical and permanent change in his or her life. It's possible to modify certain habits, but eventually the old habits will come back. Only the Holy Spirit has the power to transform a life and produce changes that will last.

For many years we thought that the Holy Spirit would only touch the lives of those who lived in holiness. But when I thought about it, I realized that it is the Holy Spirit who sanctifies lives. For me to be filled and baptized, the Holy Spirit needs to come to my life. How can I be holy if He doesn't dwell in me?

So many times I had tried to change, and I couldn't. But once I met the Lord and His Holy Spirit started to work in my life, it happened. We need to have the Comforter in us to be able to achieve holiness and receive His fullness. Through the crusades and various testimonies, God started to show me the work of the Holy Spirit in people's lives.

As I was preaching in one of our first crusades, I saw a woman walking toward the platform. She was firmly grabbing a man by the arm. He was totally drunk and could barely stand on his feet. They were walking with great difficulty—two steps forward, one step back. Finally they reached the platform. Of course, the man couldn't go away; if the woman would let go of his arm, he would fall flat on his face in an instant. I began to talk to the congregation about sin and God's forgiveness. I asked the people who wanted to receive the Lord in their hearts to raise their hands. I saw the woman lifting the drunken man's hand, encouraging him to repeat the prayer of faith. When I saw this, I thought that this was a Christian lady who had an alcoholic husband and that the only way of bringing him to the crusade was drunk. I continued to pray for the souls who had surrendered to the Lord; I prayed for deliverance, for the sick, and finally I prayed for the baptism of the Holy Spirit.

On that night, many people gave their testimony of healing and deliverance. Suddenly, I saw the drunkard on the platform waiting to testify. I desperately looked for my assistants to take him down. It wasn't the first time something like this happened, and it can get embarrassing. As I approached the man, he looked at me with a smile, and I noticed he wasn't staggering anymore. That surprised me. Then I saw him raising his hand, and when I was about to ask him what he wanted to share, I realized he was speaking in tongues. I looked at the woman, and she was jumping up and down with joy. Her husband came to the crusade full of wine and unbelief, and that night he ended up on the platform giving his testimony, full of the Holy Spirit. This man had only walked thirty or forty meters to the platform, but along the way the Lord changed him completely without any effort on his part.

This testimony shows us that to be filled with the Holy Spirit we only have to ask God to fill us with His grace. When He touches our lives, He changes us, sanctifies us, and fills us with love for Him and for the lost.

THE HOLY SPIRIT IN US

One evening, a young man who was a burglar walked by the crusade we were holding in the city of Bahía Blanca, Argentina. Something caught his attention, and he stayed. He had planned, along with some friends, to break into a house that night. But while they were waiting for it to get dark, the young man heard me talk about the power of God to change lives. We all know that those who sin are not happy about it. The majority of them would like to change, but something strong inside of them prevents it from happening. When this man heard the call to accept Jesus, he stood up and raised his hand. As usual, I invited all who wanted to change their lives to ask the Holy Spirit to help them become a new person. This young man did so; he told us that the moment he prayed, a fire penetrated his body, shook him from head to toe, and he started to cry. From that night on his whole life changed; he never stole again. When the Holy Spirit reached this man's life, he went from death to life, from being a thief and a drug addict to being a meek lamb in the hands of God.

The Holy Spirit does several things in us. He sanctifies, purifies, teaches us to love God, teaches us to pray, and equips us to serve in the church. When we yield our lives to God, we are filled with His Holy Spirit and become one with Him. The Bible says, "But he who unites himself with the Lord is one with him in spirit" (1 Cor. 6:17). Through the Spirit who lives in us we have the light and guidance to understand what we couldn't understand or discern before: "The man without the Spirit does not accept the things that come from the Spirit of God, for they are foolishness to him, and he cannot understand them, because they are spiritually discerned" (1 Cor. 2:14).

Why do some Christians live from one failure to another, from weakness to weakness, experiencing only a mediocre spiritual life? Don't they have the Holy Spirit in them since the day of their conversion? Yes, but the walk of the Holy Spirit in our lives depends on how surrendered we are to Him. He wants us to give ourselves entirely to Him, but He will only take what we're willing to give Him. When a person is full of the Holy Spirit, his fruits will show it. We may be full of God, have received His Holy Spirit and His baptism, but we may have lost that fullness of the Spirit over time. God can fill us with His Spirit in one second, but then it's up to us to stay filled.

I know many people who were full of the Holy Spirit for a while, but then the fullness diminished. I also know others who had a very simple baptism but have treasured it in their hearts and cared for it; they have practiced it and maintained it active and alive. Just by looking at them we can notice that they are full of the Spirit of God. When going through struggles and trials, they are joyful. When facing dangers, they stand firm. Those who have the Holy Spirit in their lives are those who trust completely in God and are not afraid; their works will demonstrate their fullness.

When I received the Holy Spirit, it was explosive, but then it was a real struggle to keep His fullness. The night I received the baptism of the Holy Spirit marked my ministry and me forever. It was during a meeting with evangelist Manuel Ruiz. We started to pray and worship God. In a few minutes most of the people in the place were speaking in new tongues. María, my wife, looked like an angel. She was singing and speaking in tongues with such fluency. I suddenly realized that everybody was receiving the baptism except me. From the depth of my soul I wanted to receive the baptism they were receiving. I started to cry out to God with all my heart, "Lord, baptize me or I will die!" I had only known Him for a week, and I was already experiencing incredible things.

As I was crying out to God with all that was in me, asking for His baptism, lightning fell over me from heaven. It was God's power. It threw me to the ground, and I started to speak in new tongues. I was speaking one language after another, all throughout that night. By the next day I had lost my voice, and it has never been the same since. But the Lord gave me a vision that night. I saw myself in a large stadium, three stories high, speaking to 150,000 people. I was shouting to them, trying to explain what was happening to me—the baptism of the Holy Spirit. That is why I shouted for an hour and a half in tongues. Of course, at that time I ignored the fact that God was giving me a vision of what was going to be "my call to preach the gospel."

That night, my neighbors heard me shouting aloud in different languages for several hours. They were probably very surprised when I greeted them the next day. As I told you before, I was a very important businessman, and my business and family were the center of my life. Although I had lived in the same house for many years, I had never bothered to greet any of my neighbors. That morning, several of them were out in the street talking, probably sharing about the shouting they had heard the night before. When I left to go to work, I stopped right in front of them and said, "God bless you!"

Very surprised, they replied, "Good morning!"

When I arrived at work, I gave my clients a hug; many of them realized that something had happened to me. They felt a sensation like a burning fire when I gave them a hug or shook their hands. So they asked me what had happened, and I told them about Christ.

From then on I started having supernatural experiences. One time I touched a man, and he flew up in the air, landing two meters away from where we were standing. Another time I went to somebody's home to discuss some business-related issues, and evil spirits started to manifest in his house. I couldn't understand most of these occurrences since I had only been a believer for a short period of time.

The Bible says that "God anointed Jesus of Nazareth with the Holy Spirit and power, and…he went around doing good and healing all who were under the power of the devil, because God was with him" (Acts 10:38). He is also with us. The Holy Spirit doesn't come just to help us speak in tongues or to make us fall to the ground. He doesn't come to us so we can dance in the Spirit or cry. He is a living manifestation of God's power in our lives, and He anoints us to do good works, heal those who are under the power of the devil, and proclaim the gospel of Jesus Christ; that is His purpose.

The visible manifestation of the power of the Holy Spirit was that I fell and spoke in tongues. The Holy Spirit continued, however, to work through me whenever I prayed for somebody to be healed or when I preached about Christ. This is the reason why the anointing comes to the believer. The baptism of the Holy Spirit has a purpose, and it is the same purpose God had when He anointed Jesus. The Holy Spirit comes with power, giving us signs, knowledge, revealing things to us, and helping us to stand firm in God. If we learn to depend on Him constantly and permanently, He will guide us.

There is a risk in running from one activity to another. We can become "professionals" and forget to stop to ask the Holy Spirit how to solve a certain problem or how to act in a certain situation. Most Christians, after their conversion, ask God for the baptism of the Holy Spirit. And yet, after they receive it, many are not careful, and they lose it. It is our responsibility to keep it and to increase it daily. If you have received the baptism of the Holy Spirit, take care of it! Don't stop speaking in tongues. Continue that special and intimate relationship you have with the Holy Spirit, and He will guide you every step of the way.

The Holy Spirit in the Church

Jesus knew that the church would need power; without that power they were not going to be able to minister His love and His grace here on Earth. So He sent the Holy Spirit to empower His followers to become His witnesses.

I am going to send you what my Father has promised; but stay in
the city until you have been clothed with power from on high.

—LUKE 24:49

But you will receive power when the Holy Spirit comes on you; and
you will be my witnesses in Jerusalem, and in all Judea and Samaria,
and to the ends of the earth.

—ACTS 1:8

God chose a specific day for this to happen—the Day of Pentecost. He
chose that day for His church to be born in Jerusalem. This happened
two thousand years ago. The Day of Pentecost was an important feast
day for the people of Israel. On that day they celebrated the Feast of
Weeks, also called the Feast of Harvest or the day of firstfruits. People
from many faraway places and cities gathered in Jerusalem for the
Feast of Weeks on the Day of Pentecost. This feast took place fifty days
after Passover.

The Bible says that Jesus preached to thousands of people who were
healed and delivered, and He appeared to more than five hundred
people after His resurrection. But what happened next? On the Day of
Pentecost only one hundred twenty people were present in the Upper
Room. Where were the thousands who had been healed? Where were
the five hundred who had seen Him? Only one hundred twenty were
in that upstairs room, expecting His promise. What happened then?
A sound like the blowing of a violent wind came from heaven, and all
were filled with the Holy Spirit. They began to speak in other tongues
as the Spirit enabled them. On this day, designed by God to empower
His newfound church, the Holy Spirit came to equip the church to do
the works of the kingdom here on Earth.

Soon the whole city was in an uproar. As the one hundred twenty
who had received the power of God went out into the streets of the city,
they brought the city to a halt. The learned observed that these men
who didn't know how to speak in other languages were now speaking
in other tongues. Others made fun of them, saying they were drunk.
Just imagine the scene—one hundred twenty people with their hands
raised, speaking in different languages, joyful, clapping, maybe even
jumping and dancing. Obviously, the religious ones who were present
were offended.

I don't think things have changed that much. Religious people who visit our crusades are also shocked at times. Thank God the Holy Spirit doesn't request our permission to do what He wants to do.

I clearly remember our crusade in the city of Córdoba, which is considered a very educated place. Many doctors and lawyers helped during the crusade, as well as people from different universities. But the city was shocked each night at the miracles, wonders, and thousands who spoke in tongues. More than eighty-five thousand souls came to the Lord in that crusade. Blessed scandal!

On the Day of Pentecost two thousand years ago, the city was in a commotion. Many religious men tried to stop the event. But Peter, who had denied Jesus just a few days before and who had been so afraid, stood up and said:

> These men are not drunk, as you suppose. It's only nine in the morning! No, this is what was spoken by the prophet Joel: "In the last days," God says, "I will pour out my Spirit on all people. Your sons and daughters will prophesy, your young men will see visions, your old men will dream dreams."
>
> —Acts 2:15–17

If you have been religious until now, leave your religiosity behind and ask God to fill you with the Holy Spirit. Don't be full of religion—but be filled with the power of God! Religious people will say, "Tongues were only for the apostles! The prophecies were only for the apostles!" But my Bible tells me that Jesus Christ is the same yesterday, today, and forever.

We are in the last days, and the Scripture passages that tell us our sons and daughters will prophesy are being fulfilled today. Some years ago in 1981 when my children told me that they wanted to receive the baptism of the Holy Spirit, I said, "All right, if you want God to baptize you, go to your room and kneel down to pray." So they did. They went to their room and started to ask God for His baptism. Even our little baby girl was there, in her nanny's arms. All of a sudden I heard a clamor coming from their room. I told my wife, María, "Let's go to see the children. God is visiting them." When we came into the room, the nanny was shaking. She was a new believer, but she was speaking in tongues and prophesying. My eldest daughter was on the floor prophesying. The rest of the children were speaking in tongues.

When my wife and I started to pray with them, my son, one of the oldest, started to prophesy in a language that appeared to be German. I asked the Lord to give me the interpretation. God told me to lay my hands on my wife, because she was going to interpret those words. I did this while all the others continued praying. María, who was at that time holding our baby girl in her arms, put her on the bed, and standing up said, "Soon, very soon, a great revival will come to Argentina, and Argentina will be Mine," says the Lord." My son continued repeating the prophecy in a language unknown to us. In the midst of the fire in that room, the Lord brought His Word to us and declared what was to come. We had only been believers for two years, and our ministry had not yet even started.

Many Christians laughed when we said a revival was coming to Argentina and that thousands of souls were going to come to the Lord. But that night, while God showed us His plan for our country, I said to Him, "Lord, we want to be a part of what You will be doing."

From that moment on, the Holy Spirit started to reveal things to me about my present evangelistic ministry. God told me in advance what He was going to do through it. That same year I received a vision in which I saw many books with my name on them. It was then that I told Him that I would write those books only if He pushed me.

There are many men and women around the world who declare themselves to be God's representatives here on Earth. This is not true. God has only one representative, the Holy Spirit. His Word reaffirms this. The apostle Peter, quoting a prophecy from the Book of Joel, says:

> Even on my servants, both men and women, I will pour out my Spirit in those days, and they will prophesy. I will show wonders in the heaven above and signs on the earth below, blood and fire and billows of smoke. The sun will be turned to darkness and the moon to blood before the coming of the great and glorious day of the Lord. And everyone who calls on the name of the Lord will be saved.
>
> —ACTS 2:18–21

Peter spoke to those who were looking for an explanation as to what happened on that Day of Pentecost. The end result was that more than three thousand people were baptized and remained devoted to the apostles' teaching.

God promised to show wonders in the heavens above and signs on the earth below. This is for all His servants, for His church. Are you ready to receive the signs He has promised to us? Do you want to experience His fullness? Raise your hands to heaven, start to give praises to God, and say:

> *Jesus, my soul worships You. I love You, Lord Jesus Christ. Glory, glory, glory to You, Lord! Fill me now with Your Holy Spirit. Cleanse me, change me. I praise You, Lord. Glory to You, Lord.*

Continue to pray unceasingly. Give your tongue to the Holy Spirit, and if words that you don't understand come to your mouth, don't stop—say them. Worship God. He will give you the gift of being able to adore Him in other tongues.

Lord, glory, glory to Your name.

Part Five

"DEADLY POISON WILL NOT HURT THEM…"

Chapter 11

SPIRITUAL COVERING

THE HOLY SPIRIT HAS PLACED A PROTECTIVE COVERING over His people. The following incident illustrates His protection to me in the face of the threat of death.

As a child, my mother used to beat me a lot. So eventually, I decided to leave the house. I received some bad advice, and I went to live with a group of people I had recently met. They told me that they were going to take care of me and that I would be safer with them than with my family. On the same night I moved in with them, I began smoking marijuana. Soon I was hooked on drugs.

As I used more and more drugs, the drugs began to block all my inhibitions. While under the influence of the drugs, I would get naked in front of my friends and allow them to take pictures of me. They took me to a woman who taught me how to dance and do a striptease.

Those same friends took me to a séance, promising that it was going to help me feel better.

I was in total bondage to these friends, and I couldn't get out of the relationship. They had made me sign a pact, threatening to kill me if I left.

I was getting more and more hooked on drugs. I even injected drugs in my breasts. I was arrested a few times, but there was always somebody there to bail me out. Once, in my desperation, I even robbed a pharmacy to obtain drugs.

One day I went to a rock concert. Something happened to me that night. The rock singer became my idol. I bought huge posters of him, shirts with his face on them, and whatever else I could find. His big poster hanging in my room would speak to me. I didn't think much of it in the beginning, but soon that picture had power over me.

In one of our talks, I told him the details of my whole life. Eventually I started to feel that this person was living inside of me and was in control. Some time later, I was arrested again and sent to a psychiatric center, where I was locked in a little room by myself. Even there I continued to be possessed by the rock singer.

I heard about an Annacondia crusade in the city of Rosario. I really wanted to go, and so I did. When Annacondia started to rebuke the demons, something terrible happened. From where I was standing, I started to curse and insult him. I shouted at him, telling him to be quiet.

A few days later, the person controlling me inside spoke to me and said, "Take a knife and kill the evangelist." I replied that there was no way I could do that, but he gave me a plan: "Hide the knife in your clothes, and go up to receive prayer and the laying on of hands. When the evangelist comes close to you, kill him. Don't be afraid; I will protect you."

That night I went to the crusade and went up front in the prayer line, ready to kill Annacondia. But when I came close to the evangelist, I fell on the ground and was taken to the tent of deliverance, where they found the knife hidden in my clothes. They prayed several hours for me. I renounced the authority the rock singer had over me. I asked God to forgive me for selling drugs and for other crimes I had committed. When I received spiritual deliverance, several spirits came out of me, and I confessed the whole truth. At the end of the meeting, Brother Carlos came and prayed for me.

While they were praying for my deliverance, I wrote down everything the spirits were telling me. Among other things, they said: "Annacondia, the spirits hate you." The spirits also made me draw a coffin with Brother Annacondia in it and a phrase that read, "Kill the evangelist." Today I'm completely set free, and I attend church regularly with my family.

—ANA

Divine Intervention

On the last night of the crusade that took place in the city of San Martín, more than one hundred thousand people were present. As I was going up the steps to the platform to pray for those in need, one of my assistants said, "Don't go up, Carlos; please don't!"

"Why? What's wrong?" I asked, surprised.

"The security guards have told us that among those who came to receive prayer are several armed men ready to shoot you the moment you go up on the platform," he replied.

"Don't worry," I said, "I have to pray for the sick; they need it, and that is my task. This is what God calls me to do. Something will happen to those men. I will pray for the people our Lord Jesus Christ brought here. If He wants me to pray for them, He will take care of me. In a few minutes you will see them leave the platform, kicking on their way to the tent."

And so it happened. The moment I grabbed the microphone and said, "Jesus," those men fell on the ground, demonized, and were taken to the area of spiritual deliverance. That is, to the tent. There they confessed that they came prepared to kill me. A man who was dressed in white and was a white magic priest had paid them and provided the weapons and the vehicles for them to carry out their plans. But the Lord gave us power to crush the devil's head. We do not believe in a God made out of cardboard or plaster, but in a God who is alive.

These experiences and others that God has taken me through confirm to me more and more that He works in supernatural and extraordinary ways. For instance, I have daily personally experienced and confirmed the existence of the spiritual covering. God promises that as part of "the signs that will accompany those who believe," there is the promise of protection and covering—spiritual as well as physical—for all His children.

The Word says, "They will pick up snakes with their hands; and when they drink deadly poison, it will not hurt them at all" (Mark 16:18). When this was written, there were no fire weapons, but there was deadly poison. It was the easiest and most effective way to kill a person. It didn't leave any traces behind. Of course, the effectiveness of this method lay in the fact that no antidote was known at the time.

Everything that we touch with our hands—the external—as well as everything that comes into our bodies will have no effect if God protects us. And yet, never forget that in order to obtain such covering, as with all other "signs," it is necessary to believe.

SNIPER RIFLE TO KILL

In one of our crusades in the city of San Justo, in Buenos Aires, from a vacant lot next to the site of the crusade a man with a sniper rifle was aiming at me with the intention of killing me. Later on, he himself told me that every time he aimed at me, a fog covered the platform, preventing him from focusing on the target and shooting. He could see a figure that came and covered me. This happened several times. He also said that each time he did try to shoot, the bullet didn't exit the rifle. When he aimed somewhere else and tried the rifle, it would work. But the moment he aimed at me, the same thing would happen again. After several attempts, he ended up in the tent of deliverance receiving ministry.

Such things still happen in different meetings I attend, here in Argentina and also in other parts of the world. People who are committed to carrying out the Great Commission, praying for the sick, and exercising authority to cast out demons will come under assault. When a church is committed to preaching the whole gospel, it will probably be under attack.

ANGELS SURROUND ME

The Bible clearly says, "The angel of the LORD encamps around those who fear him" (Ps. 34:7). On several opportunities, people who have come to our crusades told me that when they arrived at the location they saw angels around the pulpit, surrounding me. Some of these people weren't believers, and yet they saw the angels. These are supernatural signs of God. I always ask the Lord to send legions of angels to surround me. If they helped the prophets, they can do the same with us today. Angels are very important in the work of evangelization.

On one occasion, at the end of a crusade in the city of Mar del Plata, we decided to organize another crusade in a warehouse in Buenos

Aires, a closed but very spacious locale. It was going to be a three-day crusade. The moment I started to preach I heard stones falling on the roof. I stopped talking and, in front of everybody, said, "Before this crusade is over, the person who is throwing stones at the roof will be inside here asking God to forgive him, and he'll be giving his life over to the Lord Jesus Christ." Then I continued preaching.

On the second day, I began to preach, and the stones started to fall on the roof again. I didn't say anything and continued to preach the Word. When it was time for people to come up and share their testimonies, a young man came up the platform. Crying, he said:

> I was the one throwing the stones on the roof, and I can't believe what has happened to me. I grabbed a big stone. I wanted it to go through the roof and hit you and kill you. As I was about to throw it, my hand froze. Then my fingers went limp, and the stone fell on the ground. But that wasn't all; I felt two strong hands pushing me, and I moved forward almost one and a half meters. I turned around, but I didn't see anybody. I felt pushed again, but there still wasn't anybody there. Push by push I was brought to the entrance of this place. The last push was so strong that I ended up in the middle of the congregation, and when I wanted to stand my legs wouldn't support me.

That was his testimony. That night this young man accepted the Lord as his one and only Savior. Before he left the platform he told me, "Excuse me, can I tell you something?"

"Yes," I replied.

He raised his hands to the heavens and said in a very loud voice, "Hail Christ!" and went down off the platform crying.

That man had arrived there hating not only God but also anyone who talked about God. But he left with Christ in his life. If you ask me who it was that pushed him into the meeting, I will say that it was an angel. God sends His angels to help us in the work of evangelization.

My first crusade took place in a very poor neighborhood. When the meeting ended, I found out that the local gang leader had received the Lord. His friends thought that I had brainwashed him. At the end of the meeting, they decided that they were going to kill me.

Of course, I didn't know anything about this. When the service ended, I got into the car with my family and drove slowly back home.

Some brothers were standing at the door of the church waving at us as we drove by. At that very moment, a group of armed men came out from hiding to shoot us. Without even noticing them, I put my hand out of the car window to wave back at the brothers, and then drove away. The next day the brothers told me that when I waved at them, the armed men who were aiming at us fell to the ground.

Through this experience God teaches us that He is the One who takes care of us. Satan may want to get us out of the way, but God tells us not to worry; even if they give us deadly poison to drink, it will not hurt us. It's the sign of God's protection. When we attack hell, the devil will not remain still; he will try to get us out of the way as fast as possible.

Many times people think that those who preach the Word of God are free from attack, but this is not so. I am under the devil's constant attack, and so is my family. Nevertheless, I don't worry, because my wife, as well as my children and grandchildren, are all tied to the feet of Christ and are under God's total and complete protection.

The Old Car Was Burning

There is a shantytown in Argentina called "*Itatí.*" It's the biggest and most dangerous shantytown in the area. When we held a crusade there, a lot of people were being saved every day. One day, it had rained a lot, and the streets were all muddy. It was impossible to drive the car into the area, so I decided to leave it in a nearby area and walk. I had a very old Citroen; it was very light and very easy to move around. A group of bandits decided to cover it with gas, light a match, and set it afire. But something astounding and supernatural happened that night. Every time one of them tried to come near to the car, he fell to the ground. When they managed to come close enough to it to push it, the license plate was burning, and they couldn't touch it.

Something similar happened one night when a couple of guys broke into the tent where we held our meetings and stole some chairs and other things. Some of our assistants were very angry. They couldn't figure out how something like this could have happened, so we prayed for God to intervene.

A few days later, the same thieves returned with the chairs and other items. They told us that they were sorry for what they had done. They also said that those objects had something weird about them—every time they tried to sit on the chairs, they were burning. Strange things happened with the other stolen objects as well. They were very scared and thought that the things were bewitched. But it was God's supernatural power. I believe God has told me, "You are going to preach My power, and signs will follow. Miracles will take place, and the demons will come out. Be careful; people will try to get you out of the way! But I will be with you." I have a whole collection of weapons and knives that ended up in the tent of deliverance, cast aside by individuals who said, "I wanted to kill Annacondia."

Go Where the People Are

We didn't experience these things in the church, but out in the streets, where the devil is lying in anticipation. The *children of God* meet in churches, but out in the streets is where the *creatures of God* can be found. Many wonder why the church doesn't experience these things yet evangelistic ministries do. The answer is very simple. We are ministering in the streets, directly at the battlefront. However, we have God's complete protection. Satan wants to stop the church from advancing, but the church grows even more. The manifestations of God's power are increasing. Whenever we preach in parks, town squares, and streets, the signs and wonders are there for all to see.

In the parable of the lost sheep, Jesus tells us about the shepherd who leaves the ninety-nine sheep behind to look for the one that is lost (Luke 15:3–7). He also says that there is great rejoicing in heaven when a sinner repents (v. 10). God cares more for the one who is lost than for the ninety-nine righteous persons who don't need to repent. The heart of God is with the lost sheep, and His eyes are always on the one searching for the lost sheep. He sends His angels to take special care of those who search for the lost because they are in danger and running risks. The church knows she belongs to God, but the whole world is ruled by Satan and is getting lost.

> We know that we are children of God, and that the whole world is under the control of the evil one.
>
> —1 John 5:19

If you want to be in the center of God's will, look for the lost. That is where God is and all His supernatural power as well. Therefore, if that is what you do, you will start to walk in a different dimension.

In spite of this, the church makes a big mistake that stops her growth and removes her focus from evangelism. She becomes more and more a religion, just a custom, and the supernatural power of God loses strength. Jesus taught in the synagogues, but the miracles usually happened outside of them. There is where the people who needed to see in order to believe could be found. When Moses went back to Egypt, the Israelites had to see the signs with their own eyes in order to believe that God had sent him. They recognized him as their leader because of the manifestations they witnessed. Without signs from God we are just religious, and the church becomes a religion. The supernatural manifestations of God are signs that exist so that the world will believe and be saved. That is the reason why the church must have these manifestations in her midst.

Chapter 12

SPIRITUAL WARFARE 101

W E HAD VISITED THE CITY OF SANTIAGO DEL ESTERO TO hold a forty-day crusade. Before my arrival, a well-known priest had also arrived there. He practiced parapsychology and had traveled all around Latin America denying the existence of miracles and supernatural healings. He told people that the devil didn't exist. When I arrived with my team from *Mensaje de Salvación* [Message of Salvation], part of the local Catholic church was really excited to see what was going to happen since they had listened to this priest only a few days before. The following account of what happened next illustrates the power of our supernatural God.

In the city of Santiago del Estero, Argentina, every twenty-second day of every month the local Catholic church has some type of celebration. In October 1990 the congregation had decided to have a religious procession. They were going to be passing by the location where Carlos Annacondia was holding a crusade.

They started the procession, but something supernatural and difficult to explain happened that day. When the four people carrying the Catholic image on their shoulders passed by the site of the crusade, they fell to the ground. Some others in the procession also fell. It happened at the exact moment when the evangelist was saying the opening prayer. The people who witnessed what happened were scared, and they couldn't understand what was going on. But God had a purpose.

The priest leading the procession was so scared that he ordered the image to be taken to the church immediately, even though the crystal case around it had been completely shattered. Some of the people who fell ended up in the hospital, others in the tent of deliverance. And others stayed at the crusade meeting, listening to God's Word.

Later, when the priest realized what had caused the incident, he asked the local police to stop the crusade, but they couldn't. The meetings blessed Santiago del Estero. Twenty-eight thousand souls were saved, and many got healed. Such was the case of a woman, blind from birth.

—Juan

A Supernatural God

There was a huge commotion at the crusade when the above incident occurred. People started to crowd close to see what had happened. Some passing motorists thought there had been a terrible car accident and alerted the ambulance services. Some of our own stretcher-bearers, when they realized what had happened, ran to help. In the end, half of the people in the procession ended up in the hospital—without any serious damage—and the other half in the tent of deliverance.

If you ask me what happened, all I can say is that there was a confrontation between spiritual forces. We had no intention to upset anybody, but evidently these people were worried about our crusade. Maybe they thought that the procession would carry a message to us. But it wasn't more than a nice try.

There is constant spiritual warfare over lost souls in the air above us. If the church prevails, thousands will be saved, healed, and delivered from the devil's clutches. The church of Christ has the authority to do it. God has given us cities, nations, peoples, and villages. We, as His church, have to exercise the authority that God has given to us.

It's no use to ignore the fact that the devil is our enemy and adversary. Many believers don't even want to mention his name. They say, "I don't talk about Satan." This doesn't help at all. Jesus called his name, confronted him, cast him out, and took away his authority. As long as we try to ignore him, he will be like a roaring lion looking for someone to devour. That is why we see him destroying ministers, ministries, and churches.

The apostle said it this way: "We know that we are children of God, and that the whole world is under the control of the evil one" (1 John 5:19). When we read "the whole world," we may think it's too general. But the Bible explains this concept: "He who is not with me is against me, and he who does not gather with me scatters" (Matt. 12:30). There are two kinds of people in the world—those who belong to God and those who don't. Here on Earth there are many who don't belong to God, and our mission, therefore, is to reach them so they can know God and be transformed by His Word.

I believe this is the time to put our God-given authority into action. Many times when we try to be in control, the Holy Spirit of God taps us on the shoulder and says, "Why don't you let *Me* be in charge?" But we don't want to hear that. I wish you would realize the great things that God wants to do *in you* and *through you.* He has a specific purpose for each person. We need to be receptive and open to God and allow Him to use us to help extend His kingdom.

Many young people ask me, "Brother Carlos, what did you do for God to cause Him to give you this ministry?"

My answer always is, "The gifts from God are free. God gives them to His church to fill her with His grace." All I can do for God to bless me are things such as prayer and fasting. But I do these things so He can strengthen me and give me courage to resist the devil. I don't believe we have to pay for the things God desires to give us. He wants to anoint us and give us grace; these blessings are a gift from heaven to equip us to do the same things that Jesus did here on Earth.

The first step we need to take as Christians to please God is to be truly converted and consecrated to Him. This isn't easy. We are always ready to receive from Him, but we have a difficult time giving to Him what He asks of us. Some time ago, I read a story that illustrates this point.

A little boy asked his father, "Dad, would you fix this truck?"

The father took the toy into his hands, examined it, and replied, "Son, if you give me the missing pieces, I will."

"What is missing?" the little boy asked.

"Well," the father answered, "a wheel, the bumper, and a door. Give me those pieces, and I will be able to fix it."

The boy went to his box of toys, and there he found everything that was missing except the wheel. After searching carefully, he finally found it. The father fixed the truck, and the boy was very happy.

If we tell God, "Lord, I want You to use me. I want You to put my life in order. I want Your anointing," He will ask us to give Him those things that we haven't surrendered yet. Once we do that, He will use us. When we walk in the perfect will of God, things will happen without us having to worry about it.

Once I went to a hospital to pray for a man who was sick. In the bed next to his, a patient lay near death, but I didn't know it. I prayed for the person I had come to visit, and he was healed. Amazingly, after I left, the man who was dying got up, and he was healed. The people were in an uproar; they had just witnessed a miracle. I didn't hear about it until later when some people who were there came and told me.

When we walk according to God's plan, things happen. The anointing is very important! *The most beautiful thing God can give us is the anointing and the power of the Holy Spirit.* If we are in tune with God, things just happen. The anointing is a gift from God for all those who seek Him in obedience.

Consequently, since we are in the middle of a war, we need to be anointed by God to fight. But do you want to know who our enemy is? It is the devil himself and all his forces.

A journalist from the city of Córdoba wrote the following in one of the local newspapers:

> There is one who shouts and fights all night long with the devil. I don't know if the devil goes or is simply scared; what I do know is that he is deafened by all the shouting.

People can say whatever they want; we will fight against our adversary, the devil. First Peter 5:8 says, "Be self-controlled and alert. Your enemy the devil prowls around like a roaring lion looking for someone to devour." The devil is the enemy of God and His children.

Things like spiritism, macumba, *umbanda*, *quimbanda*, witchcraft, parapsychology, transcendental meditation, fortune-telling, and mental control have been growing a lot lately, both in Argentina and other Latin American countries. Do you know why? Because the church is comfortable, enjoying the blessings of God, while the people in the world are waiting to hear the Word preached to them.

To clarify this, I want to share with you a vision I had some time ago, the same as I described in chapter 2 of this book. In this vision, God showed me a beautiful place that I believe was paradise. All that existed was peace and happiness. But I also saw a five-meter fence surrounding it. When I came close to the fence, the crowd behind it astonished me. They were all lying on the ground, nearly naked. The heat was terrible. Some had their eyes fixed on the oasis. Their bodies looked like skeletons, and their lips were chapped because of thirst. They were extending their hands and crying out, "Please, help us!" At a distance, I could see others staggering and saying, "Please, we need help!" The wailing was unbearable.

I understood it to be symbolizing that the church of Christ is enjoying the benefits of God and His spiritual prosperity while remaining indifferent to a groaning world. We participate in important activities, congresses, seminars, symposiums, social gatherings, and special programs in luxurious auditoriums. And yet Jesus told us, "Go and preach the good news." The only business that Jesus is involved with is that of lost souls. Let's go out to the desert to look for the lost; they are hungry and thirsty for God, for the living God!

A WELL-KNOWN ENEMY

We have an enemy to fight against. Daily he tries to snatch souls so they won't come to Christ. Ephesians 6:10–12 says:

> Finally, be strong in the Lord and in his mighty power. Put on the full armor of God so that you can take your stand against the devil's schemes. For our struggle is not against flesh and blood, but against the rulers, against the authorities, against the powers of this dark world and against the spiritual forces of evil in the heavenly realms.

This tells us that Satan opposes the advance of the kingdom of God. Paul says that we do not fight against men, but our struggle is against rulers, authorities, powers, and spiritual forces of evil. We need to know against whom we are fighting. The United States must know the strength of her enemies in order to attack accordingly.

If we know against whom we are fighting, we can fight as we should. Now, we know that our victory is secure. The army of Jesus Christ is the only one in the world who knows, even before they start fighting, that the battle has been already won. So why give the devil any advantages? He is prowling like a roaring lion, looking for someone to devour, but Jesus Christ came to this world to undo all of his works, and He has ordered us to do the same.

THE KINGDOM OF DARKNESS

There are hierarchies in the kingdom of darkness. According to God's Word, Satan is the supreme ruler of his kingdom (Matt. 12:26). He rules the army of darkness (Ps. 78:49). He travels throughout his kingdom, roaming through the earth, back and forth (Job 1:7). In the Bible he is called "the prince of this world," "the god of this age," "the great dragon," or "the ancient serpent" (John 12:31; 2 Cor. 4:4; Rev. 12:9; 20:2).

Principalities (rulers)

The apostle Paul says that there are *principalities—rulers* or *powers* (Col. 2:15; Eph. 6:12). In the dictionary, *principate* or *principality* means "princely power: supreme rule." It is the highest authority and government in a monarchy. The prince or principality has power over a nation (Dan. 10:13–20).

Authorities

Paul also says that there are *authorities*. According to the dictionary, the word *authority* means "power to require and receive submission: the right to expect obedience: superiority derived from a status that carries with it the right to command and give final decisions." Satan has this right in his kingdom. The authority commands and directs all the activities and operations within his designated area of control.

Powers of this dark world

Next in order of hierarchy Paul mentions "the powers of this dark world." The dictionary describes *governors* (or *powers*) as "those that govern, that exercise authority, especially over an area or group." They are also officials elected or appointed to act as rulers, chief executives, or nominal heads of a political unit. They are therefore under the authority of those who have appointed them.

Demons and forces of evil

Up until now we see that all the positions are occupied by demons (evil angels). These hellish beings are like the officers in an army and are in charge of the operations (Matt. 25:41; Rev. 12:9).

Forces, according to the dictionary, are "a group of individuals occupied with or ready for combat." They are also a body of persons available for or serving a particular end. This term is used to designate the henchmen who fight for a cause or who are sent to fight. It doesn't include those at the top of the military hierarchy. Demons are part of these forces of Satan, who, according to the Bible, have no physical bodies, but are smart evil spirits, very unhappy and vicious.

The forces of Satan are his emissaries. They come in and dominate men as well as animals. (See Matthew 8:28–32; 12:43–45; Mark 5:8–13.) They impose physical diseases on people. (See Matthew 9:33; Mark 9:38–42.) They torment, produce mental illnesses, and drive people to corruption and destruction. (See Mark 5:4–5.) Satan has a very well-organized army, and even Jesus said that this army doesn't divide against itself.

UNITED TO FIGHT

So as we have seen, the kingdom of darkness has its hierarchies, and its forces come together to do evil. We, as Christians, have to become one under the power of God to confront and overcome the forces of the evil one. In His prayer to His Father, Jesus prayed for the unity of all Christians:

> That all of them may be one, Father, just as you are in me and I am in you. May they also be in us so that the world may believe that you have sent me.
>
> —JOHN 17:21

Brothers and sisters, we have to be united! Never mind the different denominations. We have to be one in the Lord.

THE AUTHORITY OF JESUS CHRIST

When Satan showed Jesus all the kingdoms of this world to tempt Him, he took Him to a high place and said, "I will give you all their authority and splendor, for it has been given to me, and I can give it to anyone I want to" (Luke 4:6). Jesus, not rejecting what just had been said, looked at what was offered to Him and answered with words from the Scriptures: "It is written: 'Worship the Lord your God, and serve him only'" (Matt. 4:10). Satan said that the kingdoms had been given to him. But by whom were they given? God? No way. Satan received the kingdoms, but not from God's hands. So, then, from whose hands did he receive them?

Let's read Genesis 1:28 and examine the blessing that God gave to man when He gave him the authority to rule over and subdue the earth. We know that the word *ruler* means "one that exercises authority, command, or dominating influence." When God told man to rule over the earth, He also meant that everything belonged to him.

Adam was the crown of all creation, but when he disobeyed, the devil, who was roaming around the earth looking for someone to devour, took away his authority and his right to possess the earth. Adam, by sinning, gave Satan his authority. This helps us to understand that the devil does have power and authority and that we are here to fight against him and take from him all the souls he's holding in his clutches. We have to take them in the name of Jesus, or Satan will not let them go.

We have examined some of these things in chapter 3, but let's look at some of these points again so we can get a better understanding.

We all agree that man lost his power and authority over the earth, but Jesus paid the debt. When He was resurrected, He canceled the mortgage and now has the right to demand possession of the earth. That authority enables us to say, "Devil, let go of that which is not yours." We take it away from him in the name of Jesus of Nazareth. Satan is usurping the earth, but we have the power to take things away from him with the authority that comes from God.

Can we fight against the forces of evil with natural weapons—machine guns or atomic bombs? No, we can't. But we have something more powerful; we have the Holy Spirit and the anointing of God. That is more valuable than all the nuclear bombs put together.

How should we fight? Just as Daniel did, to whom the man of God said, "Do not be afraid, Daniel. Since the first day that you set your mind to gain understanding and to humble yourself before your God, your words were heard, and I have come in response to them" (Dan. 10:12).

Daniel was praying with understanding because he realized who his enemy was. But still the resistance of the prince of Persia lasted twenty-one days because of the opposition of the evil principalities.

I wonder what Daniel's words were. I can see him lying on the floor saying, "Listen to me, Satan; let go of this city. Let go of this nation." I imagine that he ordered the devil, in the power and the authority of the Holy Spirit that was over him, to let go of all who were under his control.

We sometimes demand something for two or three days, and then we stop. We have to snatch out of the devil's hands all that he took away from us. We need to be firm and consistent in our prayers. Think about all the battles that are being fought to release answers to prayers. If Satan has taken away your son, and he is now lost in the world, tell Satan this: "Listen to me, Satan; in the name of Jesus, let him go. I command you to let him go in the name of Jesus." Continue to pray and testify with your life until the devil lets him go. Our struggle is against evil forces, powers, and authorities, not against men.

During a crusade in Santiago del Estero, while I was praying with a group of brothers, God gave me a new vision. I saw a large group of dwarfs dressed as Roman soldiers who were running from one place to another. Their armor resembled that of Roman armor. They were trampling weapons lying on the ground and were bumping into each other. I couldn't understand what God was showing me. So I asked Him, "Lord, what is this? Show me; I don't understand."

"What you see here are the devil's forces," He answered.

"Yes...but why are they bumping into each other like that?" I asked.

His answer was: "What happens when an army loses its general? They don't know where to go. So this is what's happening; they just don't know where to go."

I had one more question: "Why are the weapons lying on the floor?"

"When an army has been defeated, they throw their weapons on the ground and run away scared. If an army runs away carrying its weapons, it means it's ready to attack again. But the strongman is tied up, and his forces are defeated. I have opened the way!" He responded.

Now you will understand why, after the terrible spiritual warfare we had in Santiago del Estero, twenty-six thousand people out of the two hundred thousand who live in that province gave their lives to the Lord. The devil was defeated!

Satan has blinded the minds of unbelievers. When the gospel is veiled, it is veiled to those who are perishing (2 Cor. 4:3). So what can we do? We will get on our knees and say, "Listen to me, Satan; spirit of unbelief, let go of the minds you have taken in the name of Jesus of Nazareth." This is the most effective thing we can do.

My first crusades were in the shantytowns. I was known as the "shantytowns' pastor." Men who knew the Bible well would say, "What Carlos preaches, he can only preach in places like that." I had only three messages prepared. So I could only preach for three days in one place.

Then I was invited to preach to the high-society people in a beautiful residential area. The president's daughter lived there. Do you know what I preached? The same messages as in the shantytowns. Do you know what the outcome was? The same.

It doesn't really matter what we say. What matters is the work of the Holy Spirit in people. Even if I give somebody a car or a motorcycle as a gift, that person will not convert. It isn't with arguments or words of human wisdom that we will bring a soul to the Lord. When the church, in the name of Jesus, snatches out of the devil's hands what he has taken away, as soon as the evil spirit leaves, people will be able to understand the light of the gospel. This light will shine in their lives. If we practice this method, thousands of souls will come to the Lord.

Chapter 13

SPIRITUAL WARFARE 102

IN 1987, WHILE I WAS IN LOS ANGELES, A MEXICAN PASTOR came to see me. He said, "Brother, a year ago I had a vision. Today I have come to share it with you. While I was sleeping, God lifted me up and took me flying over the whole American continent. As I was flying over the different South American countries, I passed over Argentina. It was completely silent! I'm not sure what city I saw, but I supposed it was Buenos Aires. So I asked the Lord, 'Why is it so silent here?' His answer was, 'It's because the strongman is bound, and the church has attained the victory.'"

Then he added, "The Lord has also told me this: 'Carlos's ministry is the same as the church's ministry. If the church believed in Me, in My name, they would drive out demons, speak in new tongues, lay hands on the sick, and they would be healed.' The Lord told me this, and I needed to pass it on to you."

The ministry of the church of Jesus Christ is the one we need to exercise here on Earth. If we do, the sick will be healed, demons will be cast out, and the power of God will be manifest in people's lives.

That ministry is the one we are trying to show you through the pages of this book. These signs will accompany those who believe, not those who follow Carlos Annacondia or the pastor of their church. The Bible says that these signs will follow those *who believe,* and we are those who believe. If we don't take all those things the devil is holding in his clutches, we are lost. He has dominion over the television, the radio, and the media. But if the media are in his clutches, how do we take them away? In the first place, we need to pray and intercede day and night. We have to command Satan to let go of the media in the name of Jesus.

Remember our story in chapter 3 about the big crusade in 1992? That was in Tucumán, where we didn't just broadcast the meeting but actually had a simultaneous broadcast. Four stations were there, two of them television—the two most important television stations in the city. We had the media in our hands. I told my co-workers, "We are only going to broadcast through channel five. We'll leave the other one alone, so they can't say that we are upsetting the whole city." So we had a simultaneous radio and television broadcast. But the other television channel, the one we hadn't occupied, had a problem with the antenna and couldn't broadcast any programs that evening. So that night, all that people could listen to was the Word of God.

Do you think perhaps the devil placed the media into our hands because we were good? I don't think so. Most probably he was upset, telling his forces something like this, "What have you done? Why did you let go of the media? Look now at what these Christians are doing!" The devil was defeated that night. And as a result, all the people in Tucumán saw and heard the Word of God. That had nothing to do with Carlos Annacondia or the money we paid (which ended up being only 30 percent of the total they had originally asked for). The devil came to this world to steal, and he took the media away from us. He came to kill and destroy, and he daily destroys families and marriages. But we have this assurance in Jesus Christ: "The reason the Son of God appeared was to destroy the devil's work" (1 John 3:8).

That night in the crusade, I saw men who came directly from their homes. They had been watching television and had received a call to come. Some were wearing only their pants and no shirt; others were in their pajamas and slippers. When they heard the message, they just left and came. Also, four young drug addicts who were about to commit suicide came for help. As soon as they entered the tent of deliverance, they received ministry and were delivered.

All this occurred because the Word of God had been broadcast through radio and television. Three times the meeting was broadcast on television. We didn't hit the devil on the head once, but three times.

It was in that crusade that, as we shared in chapter 3, the little boy with Down syndrome was healed. I don't remember what my message was that day, but that mother believed and said, "Lord, here is my son; what can You do for him?"

That mother cried out to God on behalf of her son in front of her television set. At that same moment, according to her testimony, the child started to stand straight, his features changed, his feet were corrected, and his mind was healed. Afterward, she took her son to the doctor, who diagnosed a complete healing.

The devil will not release the media if we don't take them away from him declaring war in the name of Jesus Christ, saying, *"Listen to me, Satan! Let go of my city, let go of my neighborhood, let go of the media, and let go of my country in the name of Jesus Christ!"*

The church has power and authority to pick up snakes and scorpions with her hands, and nothing will harm her. This is an important truth. I've shared with you how many times people have tried to kill me, but glory to God, the Holy Spirit and the angels of the Lord were always there to protect me. After having to turn so many nests of evil snakes upside down, I can assure you now that nothing can hurt us.

Now, what was the outcome of this great crusade in Tucumán? As you may remember, we were not allowed to hold our meetings downtown, so we moved to the suburbs. People had to walk three or four kilometers to get to the place. It was a difficult location. There were only two bus routes. That piece of land was right by a lake that would easily flood when it rained. And that happened one night! While in the meeting, I could see the water coming into the tent and rising up to our ankles. But still the results were incredible. I'm not sure how many people live in that city, but I'm sure that practically all of them heard the Word and the message of God, since almost thirty thousand people accepted Jesus Christ as their Lord.

"The Annacondia Phenomenon"

During some meetings in Bolivia, we had a lot of trouble with the devil. And yet, God gave us great victory. A Bolivian newspaper published a report that included a picture of me praying. The article's title was "The Annacondia Phenomenon." It said the following:

Every night we are being amazed by the presence of the evangelist preacher, Carlos Annacondia, who appears on various TV channels gathering thousands of believers. These people apparently expect a miracle to occur in their lives. We have been witnesses to faintings and acts of hysteria among believers. What does this phenomenon mean? Miracle, collective hypnosis or....Besides, Annacondia is an excellent social communicator and knows how to reach his followers. The majority of TV channels after 10:30 p.m. have been showing a one-hour program of his preaching. He surely has the financial resources to pay for daily airtime during prime-time hours. And what does the Catholic church say about this phenomenon?

They must have gone crazy, thinking, "Where did this man get the money? This is surely costing him a fortune." But in reality, my dear brothers and sisters, I hadn't paid a cent for all those hours on television. What we did do was pray and take the media away from the devil's clutches. We found out that the richest people in town were the ones paying for the most expensive ads in the newspapers. Well, the same with TV commercials. I could tell you many stories like this so you could understand that the gospel is not a matter of talk but of the power of God.

Before my conversion, I used to contract advertising slots on the radio to promote my business. So I was connected to many people who worked in radio stations. When I met God I said, "Now that I am a believer, I will go to the radio stations to buy airtime for Pastor Jorge Gomelsky to preach." I went to several of them, but you know what? They laughed at me and said, "No! To preach the gospel we have our own Catholic bishop who is our spiritual advisor, and he is in charge of the radio programs." I encountered a closed door everywhere I went, even though I had thought it was going to be an easy task. I had to find a solution, so I decided to travel to Uruguay, to a radio station called "Real." There I was able to buy a slot. The people in Argentina could listen to our program, but only with a short-wave radio. We still did it with joy and enthusiasm. We broadcast the program for four consecutive years.

Now think of this: In 1980 I went to ask for a five-minute slot on the radio, and I was rejected. Then four years later, they called me and asked me if I needed airtime. They gave me five hours of airtime to preach the gospel. And it wasn't just any obscure radio station; it was one of the most popular ones in the country.

Something had happened in Argentina! The devil had to release the media because the church started to claim them and to command him to let go of the media in the name of Jesus Christ. This was not a coincidence—nothing is a coincidence with God. He has a purpose and a plan. But we are the ones who need to demand what we need for God's work, be it a church building, a meeting center, or a radio program. Whatever is not in the hands of the church we need to ask God for, and then we must take it away from the devil in the name of Jesus Christ.

For a long time now the church has broadcast her programs every night on the most important radio stations in the country. Every day the Word of God is broadcast to hundreds of listeners. Today Argentina has hundreds of evangelical radio stations all over the country.

As the church of Jesus Christ, our responsibility is to expose our enemy. We are members of the army of God, strongly united in love with the whole body of Christ to fight in an organized manner. Together we respond to the leading of the commander in chief of the heavenly army, Jesus Christ. We know, besides, that we have the help of the Holy Spirit, who guides us in all things and equips us to be victorious in every battle we fight (Matt. 12:28).

It is certainly true that our enemy, the devil, is intelligent and experienced. Although he can't know our feelings or our thoughts, his army is united and well organized. It is said that the devil knows a lot simply because he is so old. So maybe he knows that our weakness is our lack of unity, which prevents us from having a strong and well-united army. But we have a real advantage. We are the only army in the whole world who knows, even before starting to fight, that the battle has already been won. This is because Jesus Christ has already given us the victory when He defeated our enemy at the cross of Calvary (Heb. 2:14).

You may be wondering why the devil still has the lead if the battle has been won. That's because we, as the church, have not considered him our worse enemy. We have been concerned with building big and beautiful churches and have forgotten that there is an enemy out there who wants to destroy us. He knows he is defeated; he believes in the power of God and trembles. Therefore he doesn't come out in the open, but he hides. So we have to look for him, locate him where he is working in the darkness, find him, and defeat him in the name of Jesus "in order that Satan might not outwit us. For we are not unaware of his schemes" (2 Cor. 2:11).

This is sometimes the reason why the church feels discouraged and defeated. She hasn't confronted her enemy. She remains indifferent all the while Satan is making his incursions into the church of Jesus Christ. We have to confront our enemy and remind him that the blood of Christ has already defeated him.

I don't advise anyone to confront the demons in a particular place before having addressed the area's strongman first. He is the one who coordinates the strategic and tactical operations of the spiritual forces of evil. Once we have bound and cast out the strongman of that area, along with the evil angels that follow him, the demons are left unprotected and vulnerable to our attack and to the attack of God's angels who are helping us to fight. These angels of light are our helpers, and they participate in the conquest of the kingdom of God. When the demons lose their leader and their air support, they flee in fear and confusion.

There are many demons among Satan's forces. (See Matthew 12:26–27; 25:41.) If we defeat only a few of them, the power of their attack will not be diminished. But if we go against the prince, the power, and the ruler, in the name of Jesus, we disturb the forces. And so, when the Spirit of God falls with power on the demons, they will disperse and flee in terror. To attack the head of the army of darkness is not a superstition or fantasy. We have proven this in every one of our crusade meetings. From the beginning we have always tried to crush the serpent's head first to remove all authority and intelligence from him in order to neutralize the combative effectiveness of his body.

I had an incredible experience during our first crusades in the years 1983 and 1984 in the city of Mar del Plata, Argentina. The local churches had organized a crusade in a stadium. The day after my arrival, while I was with one of my fellow workers in my hotel looking at the ocean through the window, God gave us a vision. We saw three giants in the water holding a piece of glass that stopped millions of demons from entering the city. Those giants were angels who would not allow the demons to come in. The demons had already been bound, even before the beginning of the meetings.

The impact of the crusade in that city was a milestone for its inhabitants. God moved in an extraordinary way in Mar del Plata! Some people walking ten blocks away from the stadium fell to the ground under the power of God. Others manifested in buses that were passing by the site. The passengers on the buses would get them out of the bus and bring them to the crusade. The whole city knew what was happening. When the meetings were over, the people took tape recordings of the preaching home with them. As a result, demons also manifested in the houses. The heavens were open over the entire city. Everybody was coming to the meetings, even those whom nobody had invited to come, and they all would eventually give their lives to God.

Just to have an idea of what happened there, let me tell you that out of four hundred thousand inhabitants, eighty-three thousand accepted the Lord—that is 20 percent of the population! The most common healing was that of the teeth. Our estimate is that at least one member of every family had a tooth fixed by God. The media came to see what was happening, and they wrote articles on it. The crusade and the miracles were on the front cover of many of the secular magazines. There was nothing better than that vision God gave me before the beginning of the crusade so that I would know that the demons and spiritual forces were already bound.

This spiritual war we fight every day has no end. If we stop, we will surely lose what we have conquered. Through all my years of ministry I've been to many countries and have seen much religion and many structures and tradition, but very few tears for lost souls. If we want to conquer those lives, we need to fight a spiritual war daily!

Part Six

"SICK PEOPLE WILL GET WELL…"

Chapter 14

THE HEALING TOUCH

PHYSICAL HEALINGS ARE PART OF THE SIGNS GOD GIVES TO men. When I witness a miracle of healing in our meetings, my soul rejoices for several reasons. One reason is to see the transformation in people who arrive in pain but leave joyful. Each sign that evidences the power of God will indicate to man the need to turn to Him.

In Jesus's day, many followed Jesus because they saw the miraculous signs He had performed on the sick (John 6:2). The incredulous come to our meetings to see if the miracles are for real. When they witness a healing, all they can do is repent from their sins. This is the other reason why I rejoice—souls get saved when they see the miracles of God.

Read some of these exciting healings, and witness the transformations that have taken place.

DIAGNOSIS: METASTASIC CANCER OF THE BONES

What happened to my Uncle Fernando was incredible. He was gravely ill in the French Hospital in the city of Buenos Aires. The diagnosis was cancer in the bones, along with metastasis in other parts of his body, especially in the kidneys. His bones were almost reduced to powder. He only weighed forty-five kilograms.

His condition was so serious that the doctors decided against treating him with chemotherapy or radiotherapy. He was dying, taking painkillers to survive. His pain was so acute that he had to have sandbags in between his knees so they would not touch each other. Even the mere contact with the sheets hurt. He was constantly crying from pain, and nothing seemed to help.

My mother and my aunt asked me to go and see Carlos Annacondia, who was at that time leading a crusade in Mar del Plata. And so I did. I had planned to take my uncle's pajamas so Pastor Annacondia could pray for him, but in my rush to get there, I left them in my hotel room.

When I entered the stadium I saw the place filled with people and Carlos Annacondia walking among them praying for all. Every person he touched fell to the ground. It was the first time I had seen anything like it. I had a lot of faith in what God was going to do, so I ventured into the stadium. While Annacondia prayed for others, I tried to tell him what I had come for. But he immediately laid his hands on me, and I fell. I just stayed there, I don't know for how long. I don't think Annacondia heard my request, but God did. I later found out that my uncle started to get better that same night.

The next day, I went back to Buenos Aires, carrying the clothes I had not taken with me to the stadium. Nevertheless, my aunt, by faith, visited my uncle and gave him those garments. He had been in bed for three months now, unable to get up. But one evening we saw him walking around again. This was a wonderful sign. From then on, every night we weighed him, and every day he was one kilogram heavier. On the third or fourth day the doctor decided that he was now strong enough to receive chemotherapy.

When people receive chemotherapy, they usually lose weight. Not my uncle—he continued gaining kilograms. Every day he weighed one more kilogram. In the end he had regained the twenty-five kilograms he had lost.

Seeing his improvement, the doctors decided to perform new studies. They first examined his kidneys. The studies revealed that they were totally healed. Then they examined the bones. What had been almost powder was now completely solid. They finally told us we could leave and go back home to Junín.

A specialist in oncology from the French Hospital said, "This is a miracle of God. I've never seen such a wonder. This man was as good as dead; he was terminally ill."

When our neighbors saw him coming back, they just couldn't believe their eyes. People came out to the street just to see him walking by. They said, "This is the man who was almost dead, and now he is among us." He was a dead man who had been resurrected. It was a miracle of God. Because of this healing, his wife, children, and other family members started going to church. Many of the people in our church today are there because of this miracle.

Some months ago, the doctor who was in charge of him in Buenos Aires came to our city. My uncle's wife, a faithful believer, went to see her and asked her, "Do you remember my husband?"

"Of course," she replied, "how could I forget the greatest miracle I've seen in my life!"

My aunt, who is very courageous, said, "We always pray to God, thanking Him for this miracle, and now we are also going to be praying for you."

After this experience, I clung even more to the Lord. I believe that when God blesses someone like this, the miracle extends to the whole family and the neighborhood, and that's what happened to us.

—ROBERTO

STILL HEALTHY FOR THE GLORY OF GOD

Fernando, the man who was healed, shared this story:

I was feeling terrible; my whole body was aching. I couldn't rest—so much so that my wife couldn't sleep with me anymore. I needed the big bed for myself, because I had to roll in order to change positions. This situation lasted for almost a year. As many as twenty-two doctors examined me. But no one could come up with a correct diagnosis, until one of them performed additional studies. Presuming it was cancer, he sent me to the French Hospital in Buenos Aires. There, an oncologist examined me who confirmed the diagnosis: It was cancer in the bones that had metastasized to other parts of my body. I was so seriously ill that the doctors didn't think I could live more than fifteen days. I was so thin that I couldn't sit, fearing that my spine would break.

When my nephew went to the Annacondia crusade in Mar del Plata to ask for prayer, I started to get better. I had no more pain and started to gain weight daily. The doctors were amazed; they still can't believe it. Today, eleven years later, I'm still healthy for the glory of God.

In 1979 we witnessed a power encounter between the military government ruling our country and the power of God. We were experiencing His power for the first time, so we longed to preach to the lost, pray for the sick, and see them healed. We decided to go where we could find a lot of them: the hospitals.

But because of the military regime it wasn't easy to enter the hospitals to pray for the sick. I tried to go there every day during lunch break. Before going in I prayed, "Lord, make me invisible so nobody will see me and stop me." And so it was. I would go in, pray for the sick, and God would heal them. It was easy; they had faith, and I had no doubts.

THYROID CANCER HEALED

One day, a brother who worked with me and who had come to the Lord the same day I did came to see me. He told me that his cousin had thyroid cancer and was very ill. She had had surgery already; they had removed her glands and applied cobalt to her chest until her skin was burned. She was in incredible pain because of the burns; she couldn't even stand the touch of the sheets.

We went to her house to pray for her. When we got there, she got up with a lot of effort to let us in. She knew we were bringing the Word of God to her. So we prayed with faith for her, read the Bible, and told her that God loved her and could heal her.

When we left her house, I told the brother, "God healed her; I know that God healed her."

He said to me, "Amen, I believe that too."

The next day, we called her on the phone to ask how she was doing. We were sure something supernatural had happened. Her family said, "This is incredible. Something has happened to her." She was up cooking, had cleaned the outdoor patio, and had done lots of other household chores.

Then she told us what had happened. The day we prayed for her, while her husband was at work and the children were at school, she decided to go outside and clean the sidewalk. The neighbors, who knew how sick she was told her, "Come on, you have to go in and get into bed. When your husband comes back home he will be upset with you."

But she said to them, "I'm not going to die. God has healed me. I'm no longer ill."

This miracle took place at the end of 1979. Many years have gone by, and she is still doing very well. According to the doctors, she should have died back then, but God did a miracle.

BENITA'S MIRACLE

In the city of Encarnación, Paraguay, a lady named Benita shared the story of her miracle with us:

When I was thirty-seven years old I started to get sick. I was examined by several doctors, both in Asunción and Encarnación. I was in a lot of pain and had constant hemorrhages. They didn't know what to do, so they sent me to the city of Posadas, Argentina, hoping somebody was going to be able to help me there. My daughter, who lives in Buenos Aires and is a believer, came to see me. The doctor told her I needed surgery right away because my disease had reached a very advanced stage; I had uterine cancer.

My daughter decided to take me to Buenos Aires for the operation. When we got there, she took me to a crusade led by Brother Annacondia. There I accepted Jesus as my personal Savior. I believe that I received healing that evening, but I didn't prove it until the surgery.

The morning I left to go to the hospital for my surgery, I heard a voice that said, "You are not going to have surgery; you are healed." I immediately looked all around me to see where that voice was coming from, but there was nobody there, only a niece who denied having said anything.

Before surgery, they performed some more studies. The doctors saw something different, so they started to come to see me, one after the other, until finally one spoke, "Ma'am, you are healed; there's no more cancer."

When I went back home, my husband could not believe that I had been healed. He insisted I still needed surgery. I had to prove to him that God had performed a miracle, so I asked the Lord for a sign so that my husband would believe. And He gave it to me. At forty-eight I became pregnant and delivered a beautiful baby boy named Jorge. Today we all go to the evangelical church together and serve our Lord.

The Purpose of Healing

One of God's main purposes for performing these miraculous signs is to save sinners and bring them back to Him. Jesus Christ did not divide His meetings into services of evangelization or healing services. In the ninth chapter of Luke, the Bible tells us that Jesus and His disciples went from village to village, preaching the gospel and healing people everywhere. They announced the message of salvation and also healed the sick. I don't believe that the people had to be saved first in order to be healed later.

Divine healing is the process by which God works in a supernatural way in people's lives, giving them life and health. The transformation that takes place in the lives of sick people when they are healed is a supernatural and divine process.

When we study the miracles of healing described in the Scriptures, many were the result of God's mercy. Many people said, "Lord, have mercy on me." In mercy Jesus healed them. At times, crowds of afflicted people followed Him, looking for miracles.

When Jesus saw the large crowd that had gathered on the shores of Galilee, He had compassion on them because they were like sheep without a shepherd (Mark 6:34). He began teaching them many things. Jesus took advantage of His opportunity to teach that large gathering of people who had been attracted to Him because of the reports they had heard of His miracles of healing.

Let's examine in greater depth why Jesus healed. First and foremost, He healed to give glory to the Father. Secondly, He healed for the change that the healing would produce in people. Miracles change lives. And people who have experienced a miracle want to serve the Lord. When Jesus set the demon-possessed Gerasene free, he wanted to follow Jesus. But Jesus didn't let him; He told the man:

> Go home to your family and tell them how much the Lord has done for you, and how he has had mercy on you.
>
> —Mark 5:19

The plan Jesus had for the man's life was for him to be the messenger of God's miracle. His deliverance impelled him to become a great preacher of the gospel. Wouldn't you have become one?

PRAYER FOR THE SICK

There are several ways to pray for the sick. We will take a look at the one that is shown throughout this book: "They will place their hands on sick people, and they will get well" (Mark 16:18). I have had experience with this in my ministry, and I've seen hundreds of people healed when I placed my hands on them.

Laying on of hands

There is power when we touch another with our hands. Jesus healed many of the sick by touching them. It wasn't His only method, but it was the first one He used when He started His ministry here on Earth.

Let's take a look at the scene described in Mark 1:31. Jesus was in Peter's home, where Peter's mother-in-law was in bed with a fever. Jesus went to her, took her hand, and helped her up. The fever left her immediately. In the Gospel of Luke another detail is added to this account. Here Jesus bends over her and rebukes the fever, and she is healed at once. (See Luke 4:39.)

In these parallel passages we observe Jesus's attitude toward the sick woman. He comes to her, bends over her, takes her hand, and rebukes the fever, and she is immediately healed. Just a simple touch of Jesus was sufficient to heal her.

The touch is in itself particularly important. Children tend to feel safe and secure when their mother touches them. Even without a word, that little touch is a special way of saying, "I'm with you."

Now let's see, what happens if I lay my hands on a sick person and I don't really believe that the person will be healed? He or she will probably not receive the healing. We need faith to be able to move from sickness into health. We need to understand that the power is not in our physical hands—it is in the anointing and power of the Holy Spirit flowing through our hands. The Bible confirms this in Acts 19:11, where it says, "God did extraordinary miracles through Paul."

When you, leader or pastor, pray for healing in your congregation, do it believing that God performs miracles. Then that service will be special. The people for whom you are praying will recognize your faith and divine authority. This, in turn, will activate their faith in their own healing, and they will be delivered. Generally, when I pray for the sick during my crusades, I immediately ask them to do the things they couldn't do before. People who couldn't raise their arms raise them to God; people who couldn't walk now walk or run. Others touch the places in their bodies where there had been cysts or tumors and immediately start to cry. These people are putting their faith into action. Each attempt to check the reality of the healing shows faith. Then I ask them to come to the platform to share the testimony of what has just happened so they will inspire faith in others who haven't received their miracle yet.

Prayer over garments

A mother came to the crusade we were holding in the district of La Boca, in the city of Buenos Aires. Her son was extremely ill. He was in the Argerich Hospital, only a few blocks away from where we were. She brought one of her son's handkerchiefs so we could pray for him. The boy was in an irreversible coma and connected to an artificial respirator. She came in faith to pray for her son, in spite of the fact that the doctors had already declared him "brain dead." God, who backed up her sincere faith, had not.

When she went back to the hospital's intensive care unit, she put the handkerchief over her boy's forehead. He miraculously came back to his senses and started to talk. When this happened, the other women who were staying with their children in the unit started to fight over the handkerchief. I was told that as soon as they would put it on the other children, the power of God would heal them. A few days later, the mother came to share with us her testimony and to give glory to God for the great miracle they had received.

I've heard and seen many miracles of healing and deliverance such as this one. In every meeting there will be people who bring items or garments such as handkerchiefs or pajamas that belong to people who, due to their illness, cannot come to the crusade. These items are usually a blessing for the afflicted. This phenomenon is recorded in the Book of Acts, chapter 19, verses 11–12:

God did extraordinary miracles through Paul, so that even handkerchiefs and aprons that had touched him were taken to the sick,
and their illnesses were cured and the evil spirits left them.

I truly believe that a simple piece of fabric anointed by the Holy
Spirit can heal the sick and deliver the oppressed. Remember that God
wants to heal, and although many times we'll find demonic bondage
behind an illness, at other times it will be God's way to teach us to
overcome trials.

WHY DON'T THEY ALL GET HEALED?

Every night, many physically and spiritually ill people come to our
crusades. Many testimonies of healing and deliverance are shared
during the meeting. These stories inspire the faith of the people.

Some ask me why it is that out of hundreds who come to the crusades,
only a small percentage gets healed. Let's take a look at what happened
when Jesus visited the pool of Bethesda (John 5). A great number of
disabled people were there—the blind, the lame, and the paralyzed. But
Jesus directed His attention to only one. He came to this invalid man
and asked him, "Do you want to get well?" (v. 6). If Jesus were with us
physically today, we would probably ask Him why He only healed this
one man when there were so many others ill. In this case, and in all
others as well, we need to believe by faith in God's sovereignty.

I can't say that the reason for not being healed is a lack of faith. I've
seen many people come to our meetings without any faith, just out
of curiosity, and God healed them anyway. Some have come up the
platform rejoicing and trembling and saying, "I didn't believe. I came
here just to make fun of you, and God healed me."

In most passages, the Bible indicates that Jesus healed all the sick.
In some we read: "Many followed him, and he healed all their sick"
(Matt. 12:15). "And the people all tried to touch him, because power
was coming from him and healing them all" (Luke 6:19). But after
attempting to draw a conclusion from this, as I examined all these
texts I realized that all these people had gone directly to Jesus looking
for healing.

Nowadays, many go to crusades or churches to find such and such a person instead of looking for the Great Physician, our Lord Jesus Christ. That is a mistake. They want the healing, but not the One who heals.

In Jesus's time there was "a woman who had been subject to bleeding for twelve years.... She said to herself, 'If I only touch his cloak, I will be healed'" (Matt. 9:20). So she did, but Jesus noticed that somebody had touched Him with faith, so turning around He said to her, "Take heart, daughter...your faith has healed you" (v. 22). And it says that the woman was healed from that moment on. This woman, who had suffered from a hemorrhage for so long, looked first for Jesus's salvation, but she immediately found her healing too.

Many countries are going through difficult times, and people are desperately looking for a miracle. In one of my crusades several years ago, something incredible happened. At the end of the meetings, I always come down from the platform to pray for people. But that evening as I began to pray and to lay my hands on people's heads, they started to take my hand, one after the other, almost dragging me toward them. I had never experienced anything like it in all my years of ministry.

When I went back home, I told my wife what had happened in the meeting. She, with a lot of wisdom, told me, "Remember when we were newly converted? Whom did we ask to pray for us? Our bent knees were confessing our dependence on God. We never depended on anyone's touch."

If people are in search of Jesus's healing, they will surely be healed. But if they are in search of Annacondia, they will not. That's why I reiterate in my meetings, "Here is Jesus." If they are able to understand what I mean, they will be well.

On one occasion, one of my assistants asked me, "Why don't the media spread the news of all the miracles of healing we witness in our meetings?" I told him that the natural man can't understand supernatural things; he can't discern them unless he does so through the Holy Spirit.

There are some incredibly amazing testimonies, such as the case of the veteran from the Falkland Islands' war who came to some of our meetings. The young man had lost half of his skull in one of the battles, and the doctors had replaced it with a platinum plate. God formed the bone again at our meeting. And not only that, but the platinum plate also disappeared. This miracle affected not only his family but also his entire neighborhood.

Another time I prayed for a young man who was blind. After the prayer, he immediately recovered his sight and gave testimony of the miracle. I never saw him again. Four months later, when I went back to the same city for a new crusade, I saw the same young man, brought by another to receive prayer again. So I asked him what had happened. He told me that after he recovered his sight, he never went to church again. He forgot about God. He forgot who it was who had healed him. That day I prayed for him, but nothing happened. This young man had wasted the opportunity God gave him. Then I remembered when Jesus met the invalid again in the temple and said to him, "See, you are well again. Stop sinning or something worse may happen to you" (John 5:14).

"YOUR SINS ARE FORGIVEN"

I constantly see wonderful miracles of healing performed by God. But I realize that many illnesses are the result of a life of sin. We have already seen how the lack of forgiveness is an obstacle to healing. Sin can also be an obstacle.

One of the best examples of this can be seen in Mark 2:1–12. It's the story of the paralytic who is brought by his friends to Jesus. Since they could not get through the crowd to Jesus, they decided to make an opening in the roof and lower the mat with their paralyzed friend on it.

Let's reconstruct the facts together. The faith of his friends must have been great. These friends knew that Jesus could heal the paralytic, but it was hard to get their friend to Him—the crowd prevented them from coming close, and they were carrying the man on a mat. After several attempts, some must have suggested this: "What about the roof? We can make an opening in the roof and lower him through it with some ropes."

Perhaps the paralytic said, "Through the roof? Well, I really want Jesus to pray for me. I guess I'll do what I have to in order for that to happen." His friends must have measured the exact place where they needed to make the opening, and then they lowered the mat.

Suddenly, as He was talking to the crowd, Jesus saw the paralytic descending. He could perceive the paralytic's faith as well as that of his friends. So much effort to bring him there spoke about faith. So Jesus told him, "Son, your sins are forgiven" (v. 5).

Imagine what his friends, and the crowd, were probably thinking. What would you think? Jesus forgave his sins, but what the paralytic needed was *healing,* not *forgiveness.* Of course, Jesus knew exactly what the people around Him were thinking. One of the definitions of *thinking* is "to center one's thoughts on something." The Bible says:

> Immediately Jesus knew in his spirit that this was what they were thinking in their hearts, and he said to them, "Why are you thinking these things? Which is easier: to say to the paralytic, 'Your sins are forgiven,' or to say, 'Get up, take your mat and walk'?"
>
> —MARK 2:8–9

Jesus knew what was in the heart of that crippled man. He knew there was a barrier that stopped the healing: sin. Many times there are barriers between God, His blessings, and us. So Jesus removed that barrier and then healed him.

We all had barriers before coming to the Lord; I had some, and probably you did too. We need the ministry of the Holy Spirit through forgiveness to obtain healing and spiritual deliverance.

Forgiveness is very important. If people don't get rid of their resentments, they can end up going crazy. That's what happened to Beatriz, who told us the following story:

> I had a very difficult and cruel childhood. My teenage years were no different, although I thought I had found happiness when I met my husband. We formed a family and had a good financial situation, but hatred and resentment took over my heart. I tried to cover things up with money, but it didn't work.
>
> Through one of my daughters, I found out that my husband was having an intimate relationship with a young co-worker. The underlying hatred I had in my heart started to grow and overflow. I started to plan the best way to kill him and then kill myself. I tried several times to do it with knives, switchblades, guns, and other means. Even today you can see the scars on my husband's body.

I was in a deep depression. I lost fifteen pounds and became anorexic. I was always lying in bed without any strength left in me. My children had to take me to the bathroom. They had to wash me and take care of me day and night. I was never alone, because I was suicidal. I even threw myself under a passing car, and then I tried to do the same with a passing train. But I was rescued every time and brought back home. I wasn't eating or sleeping, my whole body was falling apart, and my organs were not functioning normally anymore. I had a stroke and ended up with the right side of my body paralyzed. The doctors' diagnosis was paranoid schizophrenia.

The next step was to place me into a neuropsychiatric hospital. By coincidence, I heard on the radio that evangelist Carlos Annacondia was coming to my neighborhood. He was going to be meeting a few blocks away from my house, praying for the sick. I decided to go. I had to leave my house in secret. I was in a real awful condition, so much so that as soon as I reached the place, the ushers took me straight to the counseling area to talk to me. I was really crazy, my eyes were glassy, and I would stare forever in the same direction.

When the evangelist prayed, I felt something strange on the right side of my body, and I then felt an acute pain in my head. Instantly, I felt something heavy coming out of my shoulder. I started to scream like an animal, and, according to those around me, I levitated for a few seconds. They immediately took me to the deliverance area, where they repeatedly told me to forgive those I hated so much. But I didn't want to do it.

Brother Annacondia came to pray for me. He took my hands, and looking at me, he said, "If there is no forgiveness and peace in your heart, nothing will help you." I felt that Jesus was there. Right away I understood that in order to bring my suffering to an end and receive freedom I had to forgive my husband. I did, and I was healed immediately. The paralysis disappeared, the hemorrhages stopped, my spine became straight, and all my organs started to function normally again.

From that day on I gave myself entirely to the Lord. God restored my marriage. My husband met the Lord, and today we are both leaders of a small group in our congregation. Some time ago I met with the young girl who had had a relationship with my husband and told her about the Lord.

She repented, and today she attends an evangelical church.

DENTAL RESTORATION

Once while ministering to some people who had come close to the platform, I prayed for an eighteen-year-old boy. The moment I laid my hands on his head, he shuddered and pulled back. I realized right away that a demonic spirit was in him. I asked him, "How many demons are you?" They answered me through the boy's mouth, "We are many."

I asked one of the stretcher-bearers to take him to the deliverance area so he could receive ministry. At the end of the meeting, I went to see what was going on with him. After a great struggle with the demonic forces, he was delivered.

When we finished praying for him, he told us his story. He had come to know the Lord many years before but had drifted away from Him. One day, the devil himself met him on his way home and talked to him. He took the Bible the boy had in his hand and tore it to pieces right before his eyes. Then he told the youngster, "You want money, fame, and power. I'm going to give it to you. And to demonstrate my power, I will fix the cavity in your tooth." He put his finger in the mouth of this very surprised kid and fixed the tooth with a black paste. The boy was so impressed that he sealed a pact that same day with Satan.

The night this young man came to the crusade, he was supposed to give the devil his firstborn child as a sacrifice. Satan had given him power over the shantytown where he lived. He ruled the place and had money and power. He led several local gangs. The devil also gave him a cross with a red stain in the center. He was to hold it always in his hand and invoke demonic powers whenever he wanted to. Just holding this cross very tightly would give him instant power, and that's how he held the whole place under his control.

Nevertheless, God wanted this boy to have a second chance, and so He took him to the crusade that night. When I prayed for him, he squeezed the cross, but this time it didn't work. Such was the power struggle in that prayer that the cross in his hand shot out. For several hours we prayed for him. Near midnight, he started to panic. He needed to sacrifice his firstborn to Satan that night. In the middle of a prayer for deliverance, the devil spoke to me through the boy's mouth and said, "I'm going to get rid of him. I will cause his heart to stop, and I will kill him." The spiritual warfare was so intense that the young man stopped breathing. So I asked God with all the faith I had in me to bring the boy back to life. And so He did. After this, he was delivered and gave a public testimony of it all.

When he told me the story of his tooth being fixed by Satan, I put oil on my finger and touched that place. I then said, "In the name of Jesus, I undo all the works of the devil." Something amazing happened. Immediately the filling broke up and melted. So I thought, "If this is what the devil is doing in people, I will pray that through the power of God his works may be undone." That's how I started to pray for people's teeth, and thousands of people have had their cavities fixed, some even filled with gold. God performs amazing miracles.

Satan brought sin to the world, and as a result came sickness and death. Christ came to destroy the works of the devil, and one of them is sickness. We therefore can truly believe that He will heal our diseases today. Christ carried our sins and our illnesses. Accept this and you can be healed! God can transform your disease into a wonderful miracle of healing.

I want to share a prayer for all those who need healing. Put both your hands on the place that needs healing and repeat this prayer aloud. Put all your faith in action and faithfully believe in our Lord Jesus Christ:

> *Father, my soul praises You and glorifies You. Heavenly Father, here I am before You. I pray that You will have mercy, mercy on me, in the sweet name of Jesus Christ.*
>
> *Father, begin to touch me now, my God. Begin to touch my sick body. Touch me, Jesus. Father, touch the illness in my body with Your power. Touch me, Jesus, by the power of Your Word.*
>
> *Holy Spirit, start to move in my life. Continue to heal me and to cleanse my body, Lord. Power of God! Power of God! Alleluia!*
>
> *And by His wounds I have been healed. Amen and amen.*

Chapter 15

THE WORLD FOR CHRIST

THE FOLLOWING LETTER EXPRESSES THE DEEP DESIRE THAT many of the converts from our crusades have to take the glorious message of salvation and deliverance to their families, their neighborhoods, their cities, their countries—and to the nations of the entire world.

Dear Brother Annacondia,

Greetings to you and your family. I have decided to write you so you can know my story. Something glorious happened to me, and I want you to know what God has done in my life and in the life of my family.

My name is Jagpal. I was born in 1969 in northwest India, and I was brought up in the religion called Sikhism. We believed in ten prophets and in reincarnation. But something in my heart would not let me believe in these things. Day after day I would ask myself, "What is the purpose of life if, after we die, we become a plant or an animal?" I couldn't find any sense or logic in it. There was a big void in my life. I looked for help in Hinduism, then in Buddhism. I practiced yoga, but nothing would change that inner feeling.

The years went by, and my family was always fighting. My mother was a teacher and my father a military man. He used to drink a lot, and this increased the fighting. I studied astrology and the sciences of the occult, but there were no positive changes in me. Things were going from bad to worse.

After some years, my parents decided to move to Santa Cruz, in Bolivia. There they lost all their money. This threw my dad into even more drinking. No religion or treatment could help us deal with my dad's drinking problem. There was absolutely no peace at home, and a few times I thought about the possibility of committing suicide.

On August 10, 1991, a friend invited me to a Christian crusade. You were the preacher. It was the first time in my life I had attended a meeting like that, and it was also the first time I had heard the name of Jesus. There were thousands of people there. I don't know what they were singing or saying. My knowledge of Spanish at that time was very poor. But I liked to watch the people waving their handkerchiefs up in the air as they sang happily.

When you went up the platform, the people started to clap and to raise their hands. I did what they did. Then you started to pray, and although I couldn't quite understand what you were saying, your words were touching my heart. Suddenly, not knowing why, I started to cry. And I couldn't stop. Then you opened the Bible and read from it. There was something in your voice that touched me deeply and gave me peace. I became reverent; I somehow understood that somebody holy was in that place.

After the preaching, you prayed. Suddenly, I saw a woman next to me fall on the ground. I thought she had fainted, but then, when I looked to the left, I saw more people falling. It was amazing! I had never seen anything like it!

As the people received ministry by the laying on of hands, they all fell. Everything was new to me. I had never seen anything like this in India. I remember telling a friend that only those who were weak were falling, that I would never fall because I was strong; I was from India. My friend laughed and told me not to stand in line then. Immediately, I found myself with those who were waiting for you to pray for them. I looked at the usher, and in my bad Spanish I said, "I not fall." When I closed my eyes, a thought crossed my mind. I felt the need to ask for help. So I prayed to God, saying, "Help me, God." And I repeated those same words over and over again.

Then you put your hand on my head and prayed for me. Nothing strange happened, so I thought, "Others are falling but nothing is happening to me." But when I opened my eyes I realized that I was on the ground too. And I hadn't even realized I had fallen! I breathed in deeply, and an incredible peace filled my soul. I immediately knew it was God. My whole being could feel His presence. I didn't want to leave. I could feel electricity running throughout my entire body.

The day after my conversion, I took my dad to the crusade. He received spiritual ministry in the tent, and he was delivered from alcoholism. He never drank again. Then both my mother and my sister accepted the Lord. From that moment on, my life was never the same; I became the happiest person in the entire world. The void inside of me disappeared forever.

After that thirty-three-day crusade I started attending a church in the city of Santa Cruz. There I was discipled, and they taught me the Scriptures. In 1992 I was baptized in water. The next year I received the promise of the Holy Spirit and later the call to serve the Lord. Then I finished my studies in the biblical seminary, and in 1994 I was ordained.

I have shared my testimony in countries like Peru, the United States of America, and Canada. God has accompanied me with signs and wonders. Today I'm getting ready to bring the gospel to my people, my tribe. They have to know that God is the only one who can save.

I thank God for your life, for having been the vehicle that brought me to Jesus Christ. I really appreciate you. I will always be praying for you.

—Your spiritual son, Jagpal

To the Nations

God has helped us through this book to discover and learn several tricks that the devil uses to deceive this world. We have also come to realize that the Lord gave His disciples a task to do. The message was clear, the commission easy though challenging. And, after journeying through these chapters, the following words have become more and more established: "These signs will accompany those who believe."

After Jesus appeared to the eleven disciples and gave them the Great Commission, the Bible tells us that the Lord was taken up to heaven where He sat down at the right hand of the Father. But there is something that confirms and completes the words of the Great Commission:

> Then the disciples went out and preached everywhere, and the
> Lord worked with them and confirmed his word by the signs that
> accompanied it.
>
> —MARK 16:20

These words endorse and confirm the mission of all those who are working for the salvation of the lost. The disciples went out to the streets to fulfill what God had commanded them to do, and the Lord was always there helping them, even confirming with signs everything He had told them.

Our challenge today is to understand that the enemy is creating havoc in the world. The streets are filled with people who have lost their way; they are disoriented, looking for the path we have already found. Don't you think it's about time for them to also know the truth? We have the authority, the anointing, the power, and the signs in our hands. Never forget that the Lord will be with us—as He was with the disciples—wherever we go, endorsing the work and confirming with signs and with His Word.

God's heart aches for the lost sheep. Day after day thousands of souls die in the hands of the deceiver. The sad thing is that most of them haven't even heard the gospel. Let's not allow this to happen! The Scriptures say, "The soul who sins is the one who will die" (Ezek. 18:4). We can't allow all these lives to be lost without knowing the truth.

The church of Jesus Christ has the responsibility to announce the good news. I have felt from the Lord that many in the church have forgotten the Great Commission that our Lord Jesus Christ left us: "Go into all the world and preach the good news to all creation" (Mark 16:15).

How can we preach to the lost? We preach with the truth and the simplicity of the gospel. People are tired of failures and lies. They feel hopeless, and they realize they need something. We can't just come to them with words. They don't even trust those who come with authority and power anymore. They have been disappointed because people have not fulfilled their commitments and promises to them. But the Bible says that God always keeps His promises.

The church cannot go and talk to the world with empty hands. The apostle Paul said:

My message and my preaching were not with wise and persuasive
words, but with a demonstration of the Spirit's power.

—1 Corinthians 2:4

We need to preach with real anointing. We cannot remain passive.
We need to have a message full of power and virtue from God so the
signs will follow. We know very well that if the power is not from God,
it will not bear fruit.

Christ Himself said that we were going to receive power when the
Holy Spirit comes on us (Acts 1:8). He will be the one in charge of
anointing each Christian. Then we will be equipped to gain others for
Christ. Each one of us has to do this from the place where God has
placed us, be it a big platform, a little church, or a simple workplace.
We have to preach an explosive gospel with power.

Now think, what would happen if we add authority to this explosive power? We have talked in previous chapters about the authority
that Christ has given us. I can assure you that if you preach the gospel
of our Lord Jesus Christ with anointing, power, and authority, nobody
will remain indifferent to it. The signs that will follow will be so incredible that nobody will be able to ignore them.

Accept this challenge! Don't remain insensitive to the things of the
Spirit; be ready for a change. Seek the power that God promised to us.
Seek the dynamite that the Holy Spirit will deposit in you. This power
will make our words efficient.

The Five Facets of the Great Commission

In the Great Commission given to us by our Lord, we find five points
that specifically determine the signs that will accompany those who
fulfill it.

Salvation

The first facet of this Great Commission is *salvation,* and it's implicit
in the words "Go into all the world and preach." This has to be done so
that we all can know that God has an answer for all our needs and that
He gives us the possibility to find eternal life in Christ Jesus.

Deliverance

The second aspect is *deliverance* and is found in the phrase, "They will drive out demons." We have to be completely sure that we, as God's children, have authority over the demonic forces. We can rebuke the devil with authority and confront him with these words: "Listen to me, Satan; I'm telling you to leave this person and set him or her free."

Investiture

The third point is the *fullness of the Spirit.* This is the investiture we all need from God. It is an undeserved gift received by grace. The flow of the Holy Spirit has to be over, in, and through the newborn Christian. It implies a life with purpose and meaning. The Holy Spirit will guide and direct us in our earthly pilgrimage.

Spiritual covering

The fourth principle is the *spiritual covering* that we have in Christ. When it says, "When they drink deadly poison, it will not hurt them at all," we realize that there is a supernatural covering around our bodies, physically as well as spiritually. Even though the evil forces are planning how to destroy you, your life is totally covered. This will be another sign to those who are watching. They will perceive the divine covering over your life and that of your family.

Healing

Finally, the fifth aspect is *healing.* The Lord told His disciples, "They will place their hands on sick people, and they will get well." In a world where sickness is one of the main causes of worry, where new uncontrollable viruses and destructive bacteria appear daily, divine healing is one of the signs that most attract people to our Christian meetings. As in Jesus's time, the crowds continue searching for the miracles of healing, and your responsibility is to introduce them to our Great Physician.

SIGNS TO BE IDENTIFIED

Signs have to accompany the church when she preaches the Word of God so that the world will believe. The devil, our adversary, will not stop in his attempts to destroy the works of God, but we shouldn't be afraid of him.

During a crusade in the city of La Plata, we received a note saying:

> All the witches and warlocks of the city and those of Ensenada (a
> city right next to La Plata) have requested help from their colleagues
> from Paraguay and Brazil to stop the blessing of God and to destroy
> what God is doing here.

For a moment I felt, as a human being, that fear was invading me.
But a voice from heaven whispered in my ear, "I give you power to
tread upon the forces of the enemy, and nothing will harm you." This is
the inheritance of the church of Jesus Christ.

The hour has come for us to lift together the works of the kingdom
of God, knowing that these signs will accompany those who believe so
that the world will come to know Jesus Christ, our Lord. His Word is
authority, today and forever. It becomes effective in the right moment
according to His will. And it offers the possibility to act by faith. As the
apostle Paul says, "According to his power that is at work within us"
(Eph. 3:20). The challenge for us who believe is to act with all certainty
by faith, not only to be able to tread upon the enemy but also to reach
the protection of God.

THE TIME HAS COME

In 1981 I received a message from God that said, "Soon, soon, soon.
There will be a great revival in Argentina. Argentina will be Mine, says
the Lord."

Today, after many years, we see how our almighty God has moved
and continues to move my dear country toward the fulfillment of this
prophecy. But we still have not seen all that God has prepared for
this country.

I know very well, since I have been part of it, that this is going on in
other Latin American countries as well. Great nations are mobilizing
in the midst of a spiritual revival. But let's not forget that the time has
come for us to construct the work together.

This is God's message to you—brother, sister, leader, and pastor. The
time to preach the gospel to every creature is here! And you have been
entrusted with that task.

Let's remain firm and united in Christ so together we can see fully the reality that we have only begun to glimpse: The world for Christ.

If you long for God to use your life so that thousands of people can know Christ, place your hands on this page and repeat this prayer with me:

Our Father in heaven, I come to You this day to ask that the same anointing and the same power of the Holy Spirit that moved so many men of faith and dwelt in them, that anointed Jesus Christ with the Holy Spirit and power, be on my life this hour.

Father, I receive the anointing and power to do good and to undo all the works of the devil so that the sick may be healed, the oppressed delivered, yokes be broken, and prison doors opened. Father, I receive the anointing and the power that comes from You right now!

Lord, I commend myself into Your hands. Use my life; make me a winner of souls. I commit myself to do Your perfect will in all things. In the name of Jesus, amen.

Conclusion

"Listen to ME, Satan!"

Father, my soul praises and blesses You. Father, Holy God, touch the lives of those who are reading this book. Father, begin now to break the chains of the devil, to break the ties of the devil. Alleluia.

Father, with the authority You have bestowed upon me in Your name, I bind and rebuke every spirit of sickness. Father, move through the sick bodies, change their blood, give them new hearts, and continue to move Your hand of power.

Lord, give us authority to destroy the work of the evil one, the work of the devil. Evil devil, you are defeated; there is an army raised against you, in the name of Jesus of Nazareth!

My God, pour out Your wisdom and Your knowledge on us; anoint us to do Your work! We ask this in the name of Jesus of Nazareth!

Breathe Your Holy Spirit on us and equip us. Give us Your love for the lost, for those who suffer.

Listen to me, Satan; I'm against you! Spirit of witchcraft, of macumba, of umbanda, of quimbanda, come out of these lives, out of the nations! Spirit of black magic and white magic, go away! Demon of red magic, get out of here now! Touch these lives, God. Break the chains and satanic bondage. Devil, get out!

Our God, move Your hand of power. I rebuke all madness; spirit of the devil, go! I break all magic spells; I destroy all satanic spells!

O God, Your church stands up. We receive power, power from God. Breathe on us, Holy Spirit! Lord, we are Your church, the winning and victorious church.

Devil, you are defeated. Listen to me, Satan; take your hands off the nations. Get out in the name of Jesus! And you, Satan, you are defeated for all eternity.

Amen and amen.

Appendix A

Appendix A

AN EXAMPLE TO IMITATE AND FOLLOW

I N THE SIXTIES, ONE OF THE PROBLEMS THE CHURCH HAD WAS the lack of unity among the pastors. The conversions were few because there were no experiences that had an impact on the people.

At the end of 1984, some pastors started to look for ways to become united, attempting to reach an ever-growing oneness. In 1985 we invited evangelist Carlos Annacondia to conduct an evangelistic crusade in the city of Rosario. We had two motives for doing this: In the first place, since the pastors had become united, there was a need to experience something new. And second, we had no doubt that Carlos Annacondia was the man God had raised up in Argentina—we had been at his crusade in San Justo and had gotten very excited as we witnessed God's power performing wonders.

Until then, the church in the city of Rosario hadn't shown any important breakthroughs. Besides, it was evident that there was heavy opposition to the gospel and that the enemy was strong.

The crusade with Carlos Annacondia arrived in November of 1985. On the initial days, one could perceive a spiritual resistance to the gospel message. But fifteen days later, demons started to manifest in an amazing way. There was a tent designated for the care of the demon-ized. Since there were so many, the place was full, and the brothers in charge of the ministry were working at full capacity. That night we felt that something had been shattered in the air, that something had been broken in the spiritual world. From then on we started to observe a few exceptional things that we had never seen before in our midst.

The devil, no matter how strong he may be, could not resist the spiritual authority of God's servant confronting him. Incredible numbers of people, overflowing our tents every night, started to come to the crusade. Every time they would hear the call to accept Christ, they would respond to it by running to the front, broken and crying.

This glory went on for forty-five days, ending because Brother Anna-condia had to travel to another city. If it had continued, we can't even imagine what would have happened!

Immediately after this crusade, we saw the results. There was an evangelistic explosion. The churches in Rosario experienced an incredible growth since they continued in the spirit of the crusade.

I remember two unforgettable events. The first one happened in our church: *Santuario de Fe* [Sanctuary of Faith]. We came out of the building and held a crusade outdoors. We did this every night for six consecutive months. The congregation grew to such an extent that we couldn't return to the building. We had to buy a new piece of land and build the new *Templo Santuario de Fe*.

The second thing that occurred was that this evangelistic awakening incited a large amount of crusades. I remember going home from work—approximately fifty blocks—and seeing five outdoor crusades. There were churches that, like us, were inspired by the spirit that Carlos Annacondia conveyed to us in his crusade.

In these new crusades we noticed something very different as we visited the new converts. Before, as we visited them, they would say, "Yes, I went, but I'm not really interested..." or "I went to the meeting, but I don't want to change my religion..." Now instead, when the brothers introduced themselves as coming from Carlos Annacondia's crusade, the response invariably was, "Glory to God!" and immediately the people would start telling some amazing story about the miracles they had received. We realized that when the people were called to the altar to give their lives to Jesus Christ, their hearts were truly converted.

Today we all know that the churches in Rosario have a large percentage of people who were converted at the Annacondia crusade. The year 1985 became a milestone, before and after the crusade, in the church in Rosario. When the history of Rosario gets written, and they describe the evangelistic work in the city, there is going to be a dividing line signaling a new period starting in 1985.

In 1992 we held a second crusade, and in November of 1996 we held the third. The impact on the people and on the church was incredible each time. People responded to Brother Annacondia's simple but anointed message. Amazing miracles took place confirming the Word. The church came alive and felt encouraged to follow the evangelist's ministry.

Listed below are some of Carlos Annacondia's characteristics, indicating that he is a worthy representative of the ministry he performs. He captivates and inspires pastors, and he is an example to follow and to imitate:

- He demonstrates his deep love for souls by his words, his call to follow Christ, and his dedication to the people. He prays for them, cares for them with compassion, without paying attention to how tired he may be.

- He exercises spiritual authority before demons or any work of Satan. He shows the reality of the power of God when he delivers people from all their burdens and from spiritual oppression.

- There are extraordinary miracles that accompany his ministry. These miraculous signs endorse the message he preaches about a Christ who saves and heals.

- His humility is evidenced in his ministry. He never wanted to be a "star." He taught us how simple and powerful the gospel is with simplicity and much love. People love him because he is an authentic and transparent man of God.

Finally, I can assure you that I have seen many ways and methods of evangelism, but none as effective as the one performed by Carlos Annacondia. I believe that it is not a method, but the sum of all the characteristics described above.

Our prayer is that God will keep him as fresh and whole in the Spirit as he was in 1985 and that God will raise another thousand Annacondias so we can see millions in our cities and nations come to the feet of our Lord Jesus Christ.

—NORBERTO O. CARLINI

PASTOR OF *TEMPLO SANTUARIO DE FE* [SANCTUARY OF FAITH TEMPLE]

PRESIDENT OF THE PASTORS' COUNCIL OF ROSARIO

Appendix B

Appendix B

COMPASSION FOR THE TORMENTED SOULS

AFTER MEDITATING ON THE FOLLOWING PASSAGE AND praying to God, I will share with you, assisted by the Holy Spirit, all the memories that could serve us as a testimony of thanksgiving and that are edifying to us.

> Jesus said to him, "Away from me, Satan! For it is written: 'Worship the Lord your God, and serve him only.'"
> —MATTHEW 4:10

In January of 1979 during a pastors' meeting in the city of Bahía Blanca, the Lord told us that He was going to raise one of His little ones to perform an extraordinary ministry. He showed through one of His servants, Nilo Ylivainio of Finland, what that ministry was going to look like. Time went by, and we started to hear about incredible miracles taking place in the crusades led by Carlos Annacondia. I met him in 1984 in a convention in Embalse, Río Tercero, Córdoba.

In 1985 Carlos Annacondia held a crusade in a town in Buenos Aires. The name of the crusade was "San Justo, Jesus loves you." I was designated treasurer and coordinator of the tent of deliverance. There I had the same experience as the queen of Sheba. (See 1 Kings 10:6–7.)

My eyes and my ears were opened, and I was able to understand what that prophecy in Bahía Blanca really meant. In that opportunity I had heard the prophecy; now I was witnessing its fulfillment. God was raising one of His little ones and giving him an amazing ministry.

After San Justo, there were many other crusades, including crusades in San Martín, Paso del Rey, Moreno, Haedo, and La Boca. I continued as treasurer, and together with Juan Dicrecencio, who was the general coordinator, we shared responsibilities in the area of deliverance. Many times we witnessed together the glory of God.

Through my experience I was able to realize that in this new awakening the gospel was still the same—yet the practice was different. We had known the power of God described in our Bibles, now we were applying that power.

The Word says that Jesus drove demons out, as did His disciples. But now *we were doing it,* and, as a result, the sick were being healed. The deaf, the crippled, the mentally insane, and others were healed as soon as they were delivered from the demons oppressing them. Even Christians were manifesting demons and had to be taken to the tent of deliverance. Although they had received Jesus Christ as their Lord and Savior, there was still unconfessed sin in their hearts. So curses, the occult, hatred, resentment, unforgiveness, satanic pacts, and so many other spirits still affected them because they had not yet renounced them. Once free from the devil's oppression, these people received the baptism of the Holy Spirit, and God elevated them to the height of giants.

Love, fellowship, and compassion for the lost reigned in every crusade. Every night there was victory, joy, and happiness present. We were equipped by the Holy Spirit to minister deliverance. Whoever submitted and listened to Him did wonders.

Carlos Annacondia's teaching was simple. Jesus had given him authority to save souls, heal the sick, deliver the demonized, and give rest to the weary and burdened. He taught many young men to exercise authority over demons and over Satan himself.

I remember a twenty-year-old girl who, when there was an overflow of people in need of deliverance, would keep the demons bound in the name of Jesus until one of the brothers became available. Today we see many brothers in the churches exercising authority over demons, but in those days it was extraordinary to see the fulfillment of the prophecy we had received in 1979 in Bahía Blanca. Glory to God!

The crusades continued, and there were cases that marked my life and ministry very deeply. I remember a pastor's wife who was very depressed. Death surrounded her. She had been unable to forgive her father, who as a pastor had fallen into adultery. She received ministry, and when she forgave her father, she was set free from the demons that had been constantly tormenting her. She was joyful again.

There was another pastor's wife who would come repeatedly to the tent of deliverance to receive prayer. She had marital problems and was tormented by an evil spirit of homicide and suicide. After receiving deliverance, she forgave, and she was reconciled with her husband and with the Lord. She then started to minister to others in the tent.

Another case had an impact on me. The wife of a young pastor came for prayer, and her story made us realize that God's children can also be afflicted by demons and can suffer the consequences of having been involved, directly or indirectly, with witches and sorcerers who have cast a spell on them.

Since the day she married when she was seventeen years old, she had stomach problems. This continued for twelve years. She was very thin and couldn't have any children. On the third night of the crusade, several brothers took her to the tent of deliverance since she had become very violent. Her husband came and told me about her, and he expressed how worried he had always been about her health. She received ministry for two consecutive nights. On the third day, a brother who was working on her deliverance said that somebody had cast a spell on her. Another said that it was a family problem.

It all seemed very contradictory. So we investigated the family. She had come to the crusade with her mother and sister, both believers. As we were ministering to her, the sister started having some problems. She didn't like our questions; she was uncomfortable and wanted to leave. After two nights, she confessed that a young man in their church had fallen in love with her sister, who was fifteen years old at the time. Since she liked that boy, she went to a witch who cast a spell on her younger sister to cause her to get sick and die.

As soon as she confessed her secret, the spell that was on her sister came over her, and she started to have terrible stomach pains. We ministered to the entire family since they all needed deliverance and spiritual healing. The forgiveness and the love of God started to flow through them all. We saw the glory of the Lord.

A year later, her husband told me that God had given him his wife back—the happy, joyful, spiritual, and dynamic woman he had fallen in love with. Thank You, Lord!

In a crusade we held in San Martín, we had a tremendous experience. A group of young girls came to the tent manifesting demons. It was a strange situation. As we ministered to them as a group, they seemed under control, but when one of the girls in particular would come close, they would start manifesting again.

We realized that there was a sexual spirit controlling them all. It seemed unreal to see this happening to girls eight to twelve years old. A sexual spirit possessed the oldest, who was twelve, and she controlled the other girls. They practiced lesbianism in their church's bathroom. When we told their pastor, he got very upset with us and informed our committee that we were seeing demons even in children. And yet, when we called the fathers of these girls (who were believers) to come, we ended up ministering to them and unmasking the demons by taking authority in the name of Jesus. It was a glorious experience.

I also remember what happened to a lady who was very thin and very ill. She had cancer in her liver, kidneys, and other organs. As we were ministering to her, she asked to go to the bathroom. Apparently, a lot came out of her body. And then, when she came back to the tent she vomited what appeared to be pieces of liver and kidneys. After this, she started to feel better and went back home. We couldn't recognize her the next day. She was fine. She could walk and was completely healed for the glory of God.

Another amazing story was that of a woman who started manifesting demons when Carlos Annacondia prayed for her. When she came to the tent, I ministered to her, and after three intense hours of prayer I was able to deliver her with the help of the gifts of the Holy Spirit. This woman told us that she had been a witch doctor, along with a partner. When she got married, she stopped practicing the occult and abandoned the partnership. But her partner, who was in love with her, cast a spell on her so she would leave her husband and come back to him. That night, we took authority in the name of Jesus over the demonic spirit that had worked in her partner, and we commanded the spell to be broken. Then the evil spirit himself told us that the spell had been broken and that she was free. Her countenance changed immediately. We couldn't recognize her when she came back the following day.

Another incredible thing happened to a thirty-five-year-old professional woman who asked for ministry in the tent of deliverance. She said she was a voodoo prophetess. We talked to her for four nights in a row. She shared how she became a prophetess, how she worked, and that even though she was leading people into death, she didn't think what she was doing was wrong. In each encounter, we gave God's Word to her, and she listened. Everything went well until she decided to accept Christ and renounce all practices that didn't belong to the Lord. Then all hell broke loose. The demon in her manifested, very upset by her decision. But with the authority there is in the name of Jesus, he was forced to come out. Then we realized how important it is to receive the Lord as our Savior and to renounce all evil practices.

I remember another amazing situation. It was in a crusade in La Boca. One night when I wasn't in the tent of deliverance, someone came to tell me that there was prophecy taking place in the tent. Immediately I felt a check in my spirit. When I came into the tent, I saw twenty-five brothers waiting to be anointed, and the "prophetess" saying, "The lord says, 'My servant, anoint these my servants.'"

When I heard her words, I asked her repeatedly, "What lord? What lord?"

She answered me, "Woe to those who resist the spirit!" This made the people think that I was resisting the Holy Spirit. When Brother Annacondia arrived and came to her, she started to curse him and to tell him that she was going to kill his children. When he rebuked the demon in this woman, she fell to the ground. She was a voodoo prophetess. That night she accepted Christ. We gave thanks to God for what had happened and thanked the Holy Spirit for His gifts. In this opportunity we thanked Him for the gift of discernment.

One night, in the crusade in La Boca, we prepared ourselves to pray in the name of Jesus against those who exercised mental control. Many renounced this practice, and after receiving Jesus Christ in their lives, they handed their medals over to us. That night, we filled a box with the different icons. From that day on, as we prayed every night presenting our needs before the Lord, we saw His glory confirming our petitions with signs and miracles.

In the beginning, several denominations accepted the ministry of Brother Carlos Annacondia. But some didn't. As time went by, almost all of them recognized his ministry. Today, they efficiently practice the ministry of deliverance in their churches, and they have leaders in charge of this ministry.

For all of this, I give thanks to the Lord—first, for Brother Annacondia, who offers himself to the Lord in such an incredible way, and second, for his family, and especially for his wife, María.

Thank You, Lord!

—PASTOR ALBERTO OSCAR BURKARDT

About the Author

Carlos Alberto Annacondia was born in the town of Quilmes, province of Buenos Aires, Argentina, on March 12, 1944. He is the son of Vicente Annacondia and María Alonso. His brothers are Angel and José María. He married María Rebagliatti in 1970, and they have nine children and several grandchildren.

In 1977 he founded his company in his hometown. It became one of the most important businesses in the country.

He met the Lord in a crusade that took place May 19, 1979. From then on he started to serve the Lord. On April 30, 1982, Carlos Annacondia started his ministry of evangelization, and in 1984 he founded his well-known ministry *Mensaje de Salvación* [Message of Salvation]. He then started to celebrate mass crusades all over the world. It is estimated that more than two million people have accepted Christ as their Lord and Savior in his crusades.

Message of Salvation International
P. O. Box 3423
Ramona, CA 92065

FREE NEWSLETTERS
TO HELP EMPOWER YOUR LIFE

Why subscribe today?

☐ **DELIVERED DIRECTLY TO YOU.** All you have to do is open your inbox and read.

☐ **EXCLUSIVE CONTENT.** We cover the news overlooked by the mainstream press.

☐ **STAY CURRENT.** Find the latest court rulings, revivals, and cultural trends.

☐ **UPDATE OTHERS.** Easy to forward to friends and family with the click of your mouse.

CHOOSE THE E-NEWSLETTER THAT INTERESTS YOU MOST:

- Christian news
- Daily devotionals
- Spiritual empowerment
- And much, much more

SIGN UP AT: **http://freenewsletters.charismamag.com**

8178